Mark

*The People's Bible Commentary*

*The Gospel of*

# MARK

## R.T. France

**The Bible Reading Fellowship**
OPENING THE BIBLE

Text copyright © R.T. France 1996

The author asserts the moral right to be
identified as the author of this work.

Published by
**The Bible Reading Fellowship**
Peter's Way, Sandy Lane West
Oxford OX4 5HG
ISBN 0 7459 2824 2
**Albatross Books Pty Ltd**
PO Box  0, Sutherland
NSW 2232, Australia
ISBN 0 7324 1555 1

First edition 1996
10 9 8 7 6 5 4 3 2 1 0

**Acknowledgments**
Unless otherwise stated, scripture quotations
are taken from the New Revised Standard
Version of the Bible copyright © 1989 by the
Division of Christian Education of the
National Council of the Churches of Christ in
the USA.

A catalogue record for this book is
available from the British Library.

Printed and bound in Great Britain
by Cox and Wyman Limited, Reading

# Contents

# *1* Introducing Mark

Many members of the first-century churches could not read, and many more could not afford to possess a scroll of their own. So we should think of our New Testament books as intended to be read aloud, when the members of the church were gathered together.

Mark's Gospel, the shortest of the four, may well have been intended to be read out in a single session. It takes about an hour and a half to read aloud, and the experience of listening to it (and still more of reading it) in this way is thrilling, as those who have attended Alec McCowan's hugely popular one-man recitations of the Gospel will know.

## Mark the story-teller

It is when you read Mark's Gospel in a single session that you see most clearly what a well-written story it is. Threads of continuity come to light, and there is a skilful build-up (and sometimes release) of tension, comparable to that achieved by some of the best dramatists.

The author must have been a popular communicator. His style is more expansive and vivid than that of the other Gospel-writers, and he seems to relish a lively scene. His Gospel is shorter than the others not because he writes concisely (where he runs parallel with the other Gospels, especially Matthew, he is often much more long-winded), but because he has limited his material. While he says much about Jesus' power as a teacher, he offers less of his actual teaching than the other Gospels. He writes rather of eager crowds and impressive miracles, of dramatic confrontation with opponents both human and demonic. He allows us to feel the disconcerting impact of Jesus on his often bewildered disciples, and to share with them the experience of having their world turned upside-down by the revolutionary values of the kingdom of God. He presents in all its starkness the paradox of a rejected and executed Messiah, of a Son of God who meets with incomprehension and hostility from the people of God.

It is all intensely moving, as the story forges ahead with breathless urgency towards the inevitable showdown in Jerusalem, where on a small local stage a drama of cosmic proportions is played out.

The trouble is that for most Christian readers it is now all so familiar that it is almost impossible for us to feel the disconcerting and yet exhilarating impact which the story must have had on those who first heard it. Let me urge you, therefore, if you possibly can, to arrange at best to hear Mark's story told in a single session, or, failing that, to set aside an hour and a half and read it through yourself (in a modern version) as if it were a novel, trying to put yourself in the position of those who first heard the story and for whom it was all so powerfully new. When you have done that, you will be in a better position to see the significance of the individual sections as we work through them in this book.

## Mark and Peter

Very early Christian tradition tells us that the Gospel was written by John Mark of Jerusalem (Acts 12:12), who was later a colleague both of Paul (Acts 12:25; Colossians 4:10; 2 Timothy 4:11) and of Peter (1 Peter 5:13), and that it was as Peter's assistant that Mark decided to record the stories about Jesus which Peter was in the habit of telling in his later days in Rome. The early writers are divided as to whether he did this while Peter was still alive (and with his blessing) or after Peter's death in, probably, AD64 or 65. It seems a plausible tradition, and in Mark's action-packed Gospel it may well be that we hear at least an echo of the enthusiastic way in which Peter would have told the stories of the man who had changed his own life and outlook so irrevocably.

**PRAYER**

*Thank you, Father, for the freshness and excitement of Mark's Gospel. Help us, as we read it, to see Jesus as he really is, and so to meet him that our lives too may be transformed by his touch.*

# 2 A drama in three acts

After a prologue which sets the scene, Mark's story unfolds in three main sections, each of which has a distinct geographical setting:

| | |
|---|---|
| 1:1–13 | **Prologue (set in 'the wilderness')** |
| 1:14—8:21 | **ACT 1: Galilee** |
| 8:22—10:52 | **ACT 2: On the way to Jerusalem** |
| 11:1—16:8 | **ACT 3: Jerusalem** |

The different geographical locations of the three acts serve to show the movement of the story towards its conclusion in Jerusalem, but there is much more to the three-act division than that. The story moves through three distinct phases, in terms both of the nature of Jesus' ministry and of the way people react to it, while the geographical movements serve to underline, and in a significant way even to symbolize, this movement of the plot towards its climax.

## Galilee and Jerusalem

Few modern readers of the New Testament realize that first-century Palestine was not a simple unity. Galilee, where most of Jesus' story takes place, was in almost every way separate from Judea (and its capital, Jerusalem). Between them stood the hostile territory of Samaria. Their histories had been separate for most of the 1,000 years since the days of a united Israel under David and Solomon, and they lived under different political systems (at the time of Jesus, Pontius Pilate was the Roman governor in Judea, Herod Antipas the Jewish 'king' in Galilee). Galilee was for most of its history more subject to foreign control, and had been dubbed by Isaiah 'Galilee of the Gentiles'. Its Jewish population were regarded by the Judean Jews as both racially suspect and religiously unorthodox. Galileans had their own dialect of Aramaic, and a Galilean Jew in Jerusalem would have been as obviously 'foreign' as an Irishman in London or a Texan in New York.

## The plot

Jesus was a Galilean, and it is in Galilee that Mark tells of the warm popular response to his ministry. It is this period of 'success' which dominates Act 1, set in Galilee; Jesus is among his own people. Of course there are doubters and outright opponents even in this part of the story, but it is significant that Mark twice makes the point that these opponents are not local, but have come 'from Jerusalem' (3:22; 7:1).

Act 3 begins with Jesus' arrival, for the first time in Mark's narrative, in Jerusalem, where he is a stranger. Here, by contrast with Act 1, apart from the Galilean disciples who have come with Jesus to Jerusalem and escort him triumphantly into the city, the overall picture is one of darkness and increasing confrontation, leading up to the death of Jesus at the hands of the authorities of the capital. The darkness is relieved by the prediction of resurrection, but it is not in Jerusalem but in Galilee that the risen Lord will again meet his disciples (14:28; 16:7). Between these two sharply opposed scenes, Act 2 forms a bridge in two main ways (apart from the geographical movement from north to south). First, it is punctuated by Jesus' explicit predictions of the fate which awaits him in Jerusalem (8:31; 9:31; 10:33–34), so that the shadow of the cross now falls darkly across the story, and Jesus' determined southward journey becomes a death-march. Secondly, the focus of his ministry now moves from public preaching and miracles to the private instruction of his disciples, preparing them for what lies ahead, and patiently re-educating them away from facile hopes of glory to the acceptance of the way of the cross, and the whole new scale of values which it entails.

## Reading Mark

All this adds up to a deliberate and quite sophisticated shaping of the story which we do well to notice if we are to hear the story of Jesus as Mark (and Peter) told it. To see Jesus in this human dimension of a divided society is to be made even more aware of how he challenges and overturns all human expectations. The kingdom of God does not operate according to the rules of the kingdoms of this world. It is a kingdom in which the last are first and the first last, where greatness is in humble service and where death is the way to life.

Was there ever another drama like this one?

**PRAYER**
*Open my eyes, so that I may behold wondrous things out of your law.*
**Psalm 119:18**

# 3
# Setting the scene

'The wilderness', mentioned four times in verses 1–13 and never again in Mark's Gospel, is a pointer to the different focus in these introductory paragraphs. They are set not among human society in Galilee or Judea, but in the uninhabited land around the Jordan. Before the story proper begins, Mark as it were takes us aside into a lonely place to brief us on what it will all be about.

## A glimpse behind the scenes

What he offers in his prologue (1:1–13) is a glimpse behind the scenes, to help us to grasp the deeper significance of the human stories which will follow. First a sonorous quotation from the prophetic hopes of the Old Testament leads us via the larger-than-life figure of John the Baptist in the wilderness to ponder the identity of the even greater one whose coming he announced. And there in the wilderness we see heaven opened, and hear the voice of God himself endorsing the mission of his Son. In the wilderness too we see Jesus in the company of Satan and angels. The supernatural dimension to these opening scenes is further reinforced by noticing that Mark, who elsewhere seldom mentions the Spirit of God, here includes three references to him.

All this provides us, the readers, with a privileged access to the real significance of what is to follow, supplying a dimension which we might otherwise easily lose sight of in the hurly-burly of Jesus' public ministry in Galilee, and still more later in Jerusalem.

## Good news

When Mark wrote his book, 'gospel' was not the name of a kind of writing, but meant simply 'good news'. That is how Mark labels the story he is about to tell: this is worth hearing! The opening verse sums it up by reminding us of who Jesus is. First he is the Messiah— and it is worth remembering whenever we read of 'Christ' in the New Testament that it is not just a name but the special title, which

*10*

surely no Jew could hear without excitement, of the promised deliverer of God's people. And secondly he is the 'Son of God', a term which Mark will record at several key points in his story, and which immediately alerts us to expect something more than the biography of an ordinary man.

## A voice in the wilderness

So we begin with some words from the Old Testament to alert us to the importance of the story to follow. They are words which take us to the heart of the hope which had grown throughout the Old Testament period that one day God would act decisively to fulfil his purpose for his people.

The quotation from 'Isaiah' in verses 2–3 is in fact a combination of related prophetic texts about 'preparing the way'. Malachi 3:1 speaks of a messenger who will prepare the people for the Lord's coming as judge, while in Isaiah 40:3 a voice in the wilderness proclaims that God is about to come and deliver his people from their long exile. The messenger and the 'voice' are heralds, forerunners of the great day of God's decisive action. It is all about to begin, here in the wilderness.

But the person of whom these prophecies speak is not yet Jesus. Jesus will not appear until verse 9. The forerunner of God is another and slightly earlier prophet, John. Before Jesus even appears on the scene, the drama has begun, and scripture is being fulfilled as a new voice is heard in the wilderness, calling the people of God to repentance, so that they will be ready for the Lord's coming.

We shall meet this extraordinary prophetic figure in the next study.

### PRAYER

*Thank you that this book is 'good news'. Help us to appreciate how important it is, to be excited about it, and to be as eager as Mark was to pass it on to others.*

# 4 The forerunner

John the Baptist was a more important figure than many Christians today realize. Indeed, in Josephus' history of the Jews in the first century there is more about John than about Jesus. He made a big impact with his 'revivalist' movement down in the Jordan valley, and Jesus several times referred back to him with appreciation. In a sense, Jesus carried on where John left off, and people naturally saw Jesus as John's successor, despite the difference in their styles of ministry.

## The prophet of restoration

Just as Old Testament prophets had often called on Israel to return from their backsliding and to live again as the people of God, so now John calls for repentance and for a new start. His rough clothes are modelled on those of Elijah (2 Kings 1:8), and like Elijah he preaches an uncompromising message and calls people to decision. Those who knew the prophecy of Malachi 4:5–6 that Elijah must return to prepare for the coming of the great and terrible day of the Lord would not have been slow to see the connection. Here in the wilderness something of decisive significance is beginning.

As a symbol of their repentance, John baptizes those who respond to his message. This was a novel and rather shocking idea, since baptism was the means by which Gentiles who wished to adopt the Jewish religion were admitted to the community of Israel, as 'proselytes'. But these people John is preaching to are Jews! In asking them to be baptized he is in effect declaring that their Jewishness is in itself no guarantee that they are right with God; they too need a new start. As they join him in the water of the Jordan they are enrolling in a new community of the forgiven and restored people of God, a true 'remnant' in whom God's purposes for Israel can be carried forward. Israel is being reborn.

# Looking forward

But John does not think that he is himself the one who will effectively restore Israel. He is only the herald, the 'voice in the wilderness'. So he points forward to someone still to come, someone 'more powerful'. John's baptism in Jordan water is merely a symbol of renewal, but the 'more powerful one' will bring the true baptism not with physical water but with the Holy Spirit. Those upon whom the Spirit of God comes will know true inward renewal. That will be the real thing.

So who is the 'more powerful one'? Christians, who know the story already, will answer without hesitation that it is Jesus—and in verse 9, sure enough, Jesus will 'come', as John has predicted. But wait a minute. In Old Testament prophecy the one who will pour out the Spirit in the last days is God himself. And the verses which Mark has quoted from Malachi and Isaiah speak of a herald of the coming of *God*. So John's language would naturally have been understood by those who heard him (and by John himself?) as referring not to any human figure but to the imminent coming of God to judge and save his people, as the prophets had so often foretold. The fact that it was in the coming of *Jesus* that his prediction of the 'more powerful one' was fulfilled suggests something amazingly far-reaching about who Jesus is: more than a prophet like John, more even that only a human Messiah. In the coming of Jesus, God comes, for, as Mark has already reminded us, Jesus is himself the 'Son of God'.

## FOR MEDITATION

*Who are the true people of God today? If John were to preach among us now, who would respond?*

*Are there ways in which we focus our attention on the outward and symbolic (like John's baptism with water) rather than on the inward and real?*

# 5 What happened at Jesus' baptism

The baptism itself is mentioned almost in passing; it is what happened then that Mark wants us to know about. He seems to find no problem in the fact that Jesus, whom Christian theology has always maintained to be sinless, was willing to accept a 'baptism of repentance for the forgiveness of sins'. (Matthew, by contrast, clearly saw this as a problem: see Matthew 3:14–15.) Probably we should see Jesus' acceptance of baptism as his 'vote' for John's programme of a restored Israel, his personal identification with the new community which John's preaching was gathering together. But that is not where Mark's interest lies.

## A supernatural revelation

Everything about this little paragraph (except for the baptism itself) is 'larger than life'. Heaven is torn open, the Spirit is seen coming down upon Jesus, and God speaks from heaven affirming that he is indeed the Son of God. Father, Son and Spirit appear briefly together on the earthly stage.

It seems odd that such an open divine endorsement should have left people still uncertain about Jesus in the story that follows. But perhaps we should not see this as a *public* revelation. Mark tells it entirely from the point of view of Jesus himself, as what *he* saw and heard, in a voice addressed to him in the second person, not to the crowds by the Jordan. It is Jesus, not the people around, who is being assured of his divine status and mission.

But we, the readers, are let into the secret, so that we, unlike the people who were to hear and see Jesus around the villages of Galilee, have a vital clue to help us to understand the significance of the story Mark is going to tell. This is not just any religious teacher, not even another John the Baptist, but the Son of God, equipped for his mission by the power of the Spirit of God. The 'more powerful one' has arrived, but he has come not in the overwhelming splendour of a divine visitation, but in the utterly improbable form of an unknown countryman, 'Jesus from Nazareth of Galilee'—about as unimpressive and obscure a pedigree as you could imagine (especially if you were a Judean)! And he appears not in the corridors of power, but as one among a crowd of penitents on the banks of a muddy river in the wilderness of Judea. God certainly has a surprising and low-key way of changing the world. He does not seem to have absorbed the principles of PR.

## Pregnant words

'You are my Son, the Beloved; with you I am well pleased'. A similar formula will be heard again (and again from the mouth of God himself) when Jesus is transfigured on the mountain in 9:7, though that time it will be addressed not to Jesus but to his disciples. Those who know their Old Testament can find more in these words than a simple declaration of Jesus as Son of God (though that must remain the *main* point of the heavenly oracle).

They echo God's introduction of his 'Servant' in Isaiah 42:1, the Servant who is to suffer and die for the sins of the people. They echo Psalm 2:7, where God greets the messianic king as his Son. And they carry a plaintive echo of the words which in Genesis 22:2 set Abraham on the road which was to lead to the sacrifice of 'your only son, whom you love'. There is rich material here for meditation on what Jesus' mission as Son of God is going to mean to him—and also to his Father. The journey which begins by the Jordan will finish at Golgotha in a sacrifice more far-reaching even than Abraham had steeled himself to offer; but this time the unhappy father will be God himself.

**PRAYER**

*Thank you, Lord Jesus, for accepting the Servant's mission;*
*thank you, Spirit of God, for the strength to carry it through;*
*thank you, Father, for not withholding your only Son from*
*the ultimate sacrifice. Help us to appreciate what our*
*salvation has cost.*

# 6  In the wilderness

At this point in the story both Matthew and Luke offer us a blow-by-blow account of Jesus' temptations in the wilderness, with the familiar threefold question and answer between Satan and Jesus. Mark merely mentions that he was being tempted, but that is all. This final scene of the prologue to Mark's drama is not so much the record of an event as a sort of tableau. Here, far from the scenes of ordinary life, and with no other human being in sight, we see ranged against each other the forces which will be active behind the scenes of the story of Jesus. It is an introduction to the *dramatis personae*, not of the earthly drama but of the spiritual conflict which will underlie it.

## Behind the scenes

The initiative is taken not by Satan but by the Spirit of God, whom Jesus has seen descending upon him at the Jordan. It is he who 'drives' Jesus into the wilderness, away from the human companionship of John and his followers. This time of hardship and of spiritual conflict is not an accident, nor even merely a regrettable necessity. It is planned by God, and as Jesus goes through it he will have the support not only of the divine Spirit, but also of angels to look after him. On the other side there is Satan, the arch-enemy of the purposes of God, and the wild beasts, who represent danger and hostility.

So Jesus, newly declared to be Son of God, now faces up to the implications of that role. The world is a battlefield between God and Satan, good and evil, and Jesus' mission will take him into the heart of that battle. He will again and again confront the spiritual forces of evil, most obviously when he must expel them from those who are possessed, but also as they work through the human opposition which will be a constant undertone of his ministry, and which will in the end lead him to the final conflict on the cross.

# The wilderness—place of new beginnings

The wilderness in the Old Testament is a place of hardship and of conflict, of testing and of discipline (Deuteronomy 8:2–5). But it is also a place of hope, the place where God first met and married his 'bride' Israel (Jeremiah 2:2–3), and the place where the marriage must again be restored (Hosea 2:14–15). So it is 'in the wilderness' that the voice of the herald must be heard (Isaiah 40:3), and in the wilderness the amazing creative power of God will again be deployed for the salvation of his people (Isaiah 35). It was for this reason that the community of the Dead Sea Scrolls set up their headquarters not in Jerusalem but 'in the wilderness' down by the Dead Sea (not very far from the place where Mark 1:2–13 is set); this was where they believed that God must begin the process of restoration in the last days.

All this pregnant symbolism underlies Mark's prologue, in which we are taken to the wilderness to be shown the real significance of the very human drama which is now about to unfold. We have been privileged to see what no human eye at the time could see, and we must not forget it as the scene closes in and the story proper begins. This is the long-prophesied time of God's coming to judge and to save his people; the ultimate conflict between good and evil has begun.

**FOR MEDITATION**

*Do we take seriously enough (a) the spiritual dimension which underlies our earthly lives and (b) the reality of spiritual evil as well as good?*

*What does Mark's way of introducing his Gospel tell us about how he thought of the Old Testament in relation to the Christian story? Have we grasped its significance in the same way?*

# 7
# The mission begins in Galilee

The prologue is over. We are no longer 'in the wilderness', but in the real world of ordinary men and women in the villages of Galilee. This is Jesus' home province, though the focus of his mission will prove to be not in the hills around Nazareth but down by the lake, some twenty miles away.

## After John—a new beginning

It was in the context of John's revivalist mission by the Jordan that we first met Jesus, but now that mission has come to a sudden end, as Mark will explain more fully later (see 6:17-29). Rather than continue a baptizing ministry by the Jordan (with the danger of being seen simply as another John, and thus possibly sharing John's fate), Jesus launches into a new style of mission, with a new message. He will not stay in one place, but will travel around the province, finding people where they are. And as he goes he will preach *good news*. Mark has already used this term in the first sentence of his book, to sum up what he has to tell about Jesus. Now he uses it twice more in these verses, to sum up the essence of what Jesus himself preached in Galilee. John's message was more negative and preparatory: repent and be baptized ready for the coming of the 'more powerful one'. Now there is 'good news of God' to be heard and to respond to. The reader knows, even if it was not yet clear to spectators at the time, that with the coming of Jesus the 'more powerful one' is already on the scene.

## God is king!

The 'slogan' which sums up Jesus' new message is 'the kingdom of God'. In the first three Gospels this phrase is constantly on Jesus' lips; it summarizes all that he has come to proclaim and to achieve. It is a phrase rich in echoes of the faith of Israel. God is the rightful king of the world which he has made and of everyone in it. But the Old Testament also recognizes that not all people acknowledge and submit to God's rule, and so the idea also grew that one day God's rule would be more truly established, and his purpose for his world brought to fruition. The 'kingship of God' (for that is what the word means, rather than 'kingdom' thought of as a place or a group of people) thus became not only an eternal truth, but also a future hope. And it is that hope which Jesus' message now triggers. No Jew hearing these words could have missed the point. God is now taking control, and he is doing it through the message and the mission of Jesus, the Messiah.

## Now, or not yet?

The kingship of God 'has come near'. Is this saying any more than John had already proclaimed, that people must be ready for what God would *soon* do? Yes, it is: the perfect tense of the verb ('*has* come near' rather than 'is coming near'), together with the equally strong perfect which precedes it ('The time has been fulfilled') indicates the present rather than the future. God's rule is already breaking in, and it is time to respond now, not in the future, by repentance and faith in the good news which Jesus has now brought. The days of preparation are over: this is the real thing.

For us, two thousand years later, the urgency of those heady days may seem far away. But the essential Christian message is unchanged. God is king, and all people are now called to submit to his rule. The good news which Jesus brought, and which this book will richly fill out, is now, as it was then, the ultimate reality to which we must respond, and which we must declare to those around us.

### PRAYER
*Thank you, Lord, for good news in a world where bad news so often fills the headlines. Help us to value it, both by following Jesus ourselves in repentance and faith, and by inviting others to come under your loving rule. May your kingdom come!*

# 8 Partners in mission

Mark has barely begun his account of Jesus' mission when he tells us that Jesus called others to share it with him. All through the Gospel from this point he will tell not merely the story of Jesus, but the story of Jesus *and his disciples*, as a team. Jesus, whom we have come to recognize as the unique Son of God and the 'more powerful one' predicted by John, nonetheless shares his mission with others. As the Gospel goes on they will often prove to be as much an embarrassment as a help, but Jesus will be committed to them, as they will to him. And when he is gone, it will be on them that the ongoing mission will depend.

## The inner circle

Later Jesus will select twelve disciples to accompany him on his travels, but the four we meet in this passage will be mentioned at the head of the list, and several times (usually without Andrew) they will be the only ones allowed to share some of Jesus' more private moments (1:29; 5:37; 9:2; 13:3; 14:33). They were, it seems, not merely assistants in the mission, but close companions with whom Jesus could share secrets. Even the Son of God needed human support and sympathy!

As Mark tells the story, the call to these four fishermen to follow Jesus seems to come out of the blue. But John 1:35–42 mentions another meeting of Jesus with Andrew and Simon (and possibly John?), which was apparently earlier than this one. They had already concluded then that Jesus was the Messiah, and so the call now to drop everything and follow him, while it was sudden and drastic in its implications, did not need to be thought about for very long. Quite likely they had been waiting and hoping for it since that meeting down by the Jordan.

Simon and Andrew leave their nets; James and John leave their father and his crew in the boat. With these deft brush-strokes Mark spells out for us what it will really mean for those first disciples to follow Jesus. The safe, predictable, ordinary life of work and family gives place to an itinerant lifestyle, with no visible means of support—and in the end the ignominious failure of abandoning their master to his fate in a Jerusalem garden. Following Jesus has never been a soft option.

## Fishing for people

So why did they do it? Of course there are many levels of answer, even if at this stage they may not have been able to articulate them very clearly. But the one thing that Jesus has offered them is a new profession, fishing for people. (Isn't it a pity that the resonant old phrase 'fishers of men' is no longer appropriate in these days of inclusive language? Of course it is correct to include women and children in the catch, but the pun on 'fishermen' does go a bit flat!) Jeremiah 16:16 talked about God sending fishermen to catch people for judgment, but Jesus' fishermen are going to save people from judgment, to catch them for the kingdom of God. Jesus' disciples have been doing it ever since. The Christian gospel is not a cosy reassurance that everybody is entitled to their point of view, and that the only sin is to rock the boat. It is about catching people out of their native waters and transferring them to a whole new life.

### FOR MEDITATION
*Have we lost something of the biblical dimensions of discipleship? What have we left for Jesus? Does he matter to us enough for us to take risks for him? Does our understanding of the good news make it natural for us to want to 'catch' others?*

# 9

*MARK 1:21-28*

# Something new in the synagogue

Simon and Andrew lived in Capernaum (1:29), and their home now became Jesus' base for much of his time in Galilee. In 1:21–38 Mark tells us of twenty-four hours in Capernaum, beginning with the sabbath service in the synagogue, and going through to early the next morning, when Jesus will set off for a more widespread mission. Perhaps we are to think of this as a 'typical' day in the life of Jesus and his disciples?

## Teaching with authority

All good Jews attended the synagogue on the sabbath, but to be asked to teach was a privilege. Jesus is already gaining a reputation as a teacher, and the reaction of the people in the Capernaum synagogue shows that it was well deserved. The thing which impresses them is his *authority*, a word which will often occur in the Gospels as a characteristic of Jesus' ministry, both in word and in action. Given what we, the readers of the Gospel, already know about Jesus from the prologue, this comes as no surprise, but for the people of Capernaum to hear a young man from the obscure hill village of Nazareth teaching with such authority was astonishing. Mark mentions particularly the contrast with the way the scribes taught, learned and judicious no doubt, but essentially second-hand and predictable. Scribes quoted other rabbinic authorities and weighed up traditional arguments, but did not err on the side of originality. But Jesus is different, bold, dynamic, demanding and exhilarating.

## Authority in deed as well as word

Verses 23–26 record the first of several stories of exorcism which Mark will tell. He clearly wants us to see this as a central part of Jesus' ministry, and one which testifies to his unique authority. Not that exorcism was a totally new thing; there is evidence that other

22

Jews engaged in it, as Jesus himself recognizes in Matthew 12:27. But what is new about Jesus is not only the frequency of such occurrences in his ministry, but also the extraordinary control which he is able to exercise over demonic forces (Mark usually calls them 'unclean spirits', whereas the other Gospel writers speak generally of 'demons'). In this story we notice how the spirit immediately recognizes Jesus as someone special, 'the Holy One of God', and assumes that his arrival spells disaster for the powers of evil (notice the 'us'); and how Jesus needs no elaborate ritual or magical formulae (as other exorcists usually did), but dismisses the spirit with an almost contemptuous 'Shut up and get out'! No wonder people were astonished, and Jesus' fame began to spread.

For most Christians in the Western world today the idea of possession by a personal force of evil, and of the expulsion of a demon, leaving the 'host' changed and restored to normality, sounds at best exotic and at worst decidedly suspect. They would much rather not know about it. But there are times even in glossy Western society when the reality of spiritual evil cannot be ignored, and in some other parts of the world witchcraft, voodoo and the occult are part of daily experience. In Jesus' world, and for Mark, the demonic dimension was as real as the divine, and a Messiah who left the forces of evil unchallenged would be of little interest. There is no sphere of life which falls outside his extraordinary authority; there is no predicament into which people may fall from which he cannot rescue them.

## PRAYER

*Thank you, Lord Jesus, that yours is 'the name high over all', that there is no power which can stand against you. Help us gladly to acknowledge your authority in all aspects of our lives, and to know that with you as our Lord there is nothing we need fear.*

# 10
# In the evening

Straight after the first exorcism comes the first healing. The contrast
is remarkable. The first was a dramatic confrontation with evil in a
very public arena; the second is the healing of a sick woman in private in her own home. But both are part of the work of restoration
on which the Messiah has embarked.

## In Simon's house

Simon and Andrew came originally from Bethsaida (John 1:44), but
now they lived in the important lakeside town of Capernaum, from
which they had until recently run their fishing business. When they
left their nets to follow Jesus, they had not given up their home, and
this was probably the house in which Jesus was based while he was
in Capernaum. There seems good reason to believe that it was this
same house which was later covered by an octagonal church building of the fifth century, the remains of which may still be seen in
Capernaum. It is not many yards away from the synagogue, and
here the small group return after the service. The healing of Simon's
mother-in-law is reported in quite a matter-of-fact way. Her 'fever'
may not have been a very serious complaint, but it receives Jesus'
immediate attention. The fact that this is apparently still the sabbath
is not commented on, though in 3:1–6 healing on the sabbath will
become a very serious issue. But this is a private affair, with no
Pharisees around to be offended!

## The end of the sabbath

Mark emphasizes the time, since the sabbath ended at sunset. As
long as it was sabbath good Jews would not carry sick people around,
nor would they expect Jesus to heal them. But once the sabbath is
over they are free to take advantage of Jesus' presence in town. They
have seen his authority in operation in the synagogue, and his reputation as both exorcist and healer is now established. In a close-knit
Eastern community the gathering of 'the whole city' (Capernaum's

population was about 10,000) around the door may not be too much of an exaggeration!

Notice the careful distinction which Mark draws between physical illness and demon-possession, not only in the description of those who were brought to Jesus, but also in how he dealt with them. Illnesses are 'cured', while demons are 'cast out'. There are a few places in the Gospels where the two conditions seem to be run together, but usually the distinction is kept clear. Demon-possession is not an illness, but an invasion, and it is dealt with as such.

## Silencing the demons

Mark is particularly interested in how Jesus treats the demons. They are spiritual beings, and so have supernatural knowledge about Jesus (as we have already seen in v. 24). There is no suggestion that what they might say about Jesus would be untrue: 'they knew him'. But Jesus will not let them speak. Perhaps he can well do without testimony from such a dubious source! But we shall see again and again in Mark's story how Jesus is careful to keep an element of secrecy about who he is and what he has come to do; the subject will recur again as soon as verses 44–45. He does not want premature publicity, however well-informed its source. He will make himself known in his own good time, and in his own chosen way. In chapter 4 this whole subject of secrecy will be intriguingly explored.

### PRAYER
*Lord Jesus, may we bring our needs and problems to you as the people of Capernaum did, and find in you healing and relief.*

# 11 Keeping on the move

In these verses we conclude the 'twenty-four hours in Capernaum' which began in verse 21. Jesus has been busy teaching, healing, casting out demons, and generally making a formidable impression on the people of this seaside town. He has, it would seem, laid a strong foundation for continuing in Capernaum a ministry which has been so successfully begun. Yet early next morning he has disappeared!

## Jesus in prayer

He has gone out of the town to find a secluded spot where he can spend time in prayer. To those who have been brought up on the concept of Jesus as God incarnate it may seem strange that such a person needs to pray at all. But the Jesus of Mark's story, while clearly portrayed as the Son of God, is unequivocally human, and in many ways shares the weaknesses and emotions of the rest of us. It may not be easy for us to envisage just how God incarnate would pray to God his Father (though in 14:32–36 we will have a precious glimpse into even this mystery), but prayer is as important for him as for his disciples.

Not that Mark often portrays Jesus in prayer (it is Luke who tells us more of that). He mentions Jesus' prayer elsewhere only at special turning-points in his ministry, and it may be that its mention here indicates an important decision confronting Jesus, regarding the style of ministry that he should develop. Certainly when this prayer is over he is ready to overturn his disciples' very natural expectation that he would build on his success in Capernaum, and instead to launch into a much less predictable itinerant ministry. Was it his hours in prayer before dawn which determined this significant choice?

## 'Let us go on'

There is something deliberately paradoxical about Jesus' response to the disciples' puzzled appeal, once they have tracked him down. 'Everyone [in Capernaum] is searching for you', so this is not the time to indulge in private meditation. There is a job to be done, a well-launched mission to be developed, an eager populace to be satisfied and helped. Yet it is in precisely that situation where his duty seems so obvious to them that Jesus declares his intention to 'go on to the neighbouring towns', to keep moving, and not to become institutionalized in one place, however needy and however receptive. His mission is wider than simply to Capernaum, and those who have chosen to follow him must be prepared to be on the move as well.

There is here a foretaste of the urgency with which Jesus will later send his disciples out in their turn around the villages of Galilee (6:7–11). The message has to be spread. That is what Jesus has 'come out' for ('out' from Capernaum in the early hours of that morning? or 'out' from God who sent him?—Mark, typically, does not say, and leaves it to his readers to draw their own conclusion).

## 'Proclaiming the message'

The Greek verb denotes acting as a herald, one sent out with news or with a proclamation, often from a king to those over whom he rules. It is the word which has been used of John the Baptist in 1:4, 7 as well as of Jesus himself in 1:14. God has a message for his people, and it is for his appointed heralds to make it clear to all those to whom it applies.

The focus on proclamation here is quite striking in view of the fact that what the people of Capernaum had come looking for was primarily healing and exorcism. Perhaps that is partly why Jesus feels he must move on, lest his task as herald becomes submerged beneath the popular demand for his miraculous power. True, exorcism is mentioned again in verse 39 (for the third time already in Mark's story), but Jesus leaves no doubt where the primary focus of his mission lies.

### FOR MEDITATION

*If even Jesus needed to spend precious hours in prayer, what does this suggest for our own sense of priorities?*

*Does Jesus' concern with proclamation rather than healing and exorcism have anything to teach us both with regard to our own spiritual focus and with regard to the church's priorities in its mission?*

# 12 'Unclean! unclean!'

The man's complaint may not have been full-scale 'leprosy' as we use the word, but it would be an unpleasant skin-disease which was regarded as infectious, and therefore made the sufferer 'unclean'. Such people were forced to live outside normal society. The word that is used for the restoration of a leper is not 'heal', but 'cleanse'. The vital issue is therefore not only the arresting of the disease, but the restoration of the person to 'clean' society. It was in token of this restoration that the person must be examined and pronounced 'clean' by the priest, and the appropriate animal sacrifice made to take away the impurity.

## An emotional encounter

Leprosy was regarded as practically incurable, so that the man's approach involves a remarkable statement of faith in the miraculous power of Jesus. What he puts in question is not Jesus' power but his will to help. The phrase 'moved with pity' represents the reading of most of the Greek manuscripts, but there is a significant minority which reads 'moved with *anger*', and it is so unusual for anger to be attributed to Jesus in such a situation, and so easy to understand how later scribes might wish to change 'anger' to 'pity', that many scholars think that what Mark actually wrote was 'moved with anger' (see NRSV margin).

But why should Jesus be angry? Perhaps over the suggestion that he might not be willing to help? In that case Jesus' indignant reply 'I *do* choose' follows naturally. Or perhaps he is more generally upset by the condition in which the man's disease has left him. 'Sternly warning him' in verse 43 is another very emotional word, and it seems that Mark goes out of his way to let us see Jesus not as the coolly detached healer but as the warm-blooded man whose 'gut reactions' run the whole gamut of human emotions.

# Testimony—right and wrong

Clearly the priest must know about the cleansing, so that the man can be duly restored to society. So Jesus sends the man off to the priest, to offer a 'testimony to them'. This enigmatic phrase will occur again in 6:11 and 13:9, in each case in a hostile setting. Is it then a testimony 'against them', showing the priests that the Jesus whom they will later hound to death is in fact the one through whom God's power has been operating? Or is it more simply that the man's appearance before the priest testifies that he is clear of leprosy? Again Mark leaves the phrase enigmatic.

But other people are not to know what has happened. The note of secrecy in Jesus' mission, which was sounded already in verse 34, is now loud and clear. But this time we begin to see why it was necessary, since the man's disobedience to Jesus' 'gagging order' has a dramatic effect on Jesus' mission. He immediately becomes the object of unwelcome attention, and has to keep out of the public eye. Perhaps it was the prospect of this sort of public response to a miraculous healer that governed Jesus' decision not to return to Capernaum in verse 38. When he does eventually return there in 2:1 the problem of unwelcome publicity will be all the greater.

### PRAYER

*Thank you, Lord Jesus, that you have not only the power but also the will to restore those whose lives are broken.*

# 13 'Who can forgive sins?'

Who can forget the vivid scene of the crowded house and the bold attempt to get access to Jesus by demolishing the roof of the flat-roofed, single-storey building? Add to that the dramatic impact of the paralysed man standing up and walking off through the crowd with his stretcher, and it is no wonder the people said 'We have never seen anything like this!' But, vivid as it is, it is not the healing of the paralytic which is the main focus of the story as Mark tells it. Indeed, the healing itself seems to come in as little more than a visual aid to reinforce Jesus' claim in quite a different area, the authority to forgive sins.

## Sin and illness

It was a widespread idea in the ancient world (and even today one can still come across it) that physical illness is in some direct way the result of the patient's sin. Jesus never endorsed that idea, and in John 9:2–3 he directly contradicted it. So it is more than a little surprising to hear him tackle an apparently straightforward case of physical paralysis with the declaration 'Your sins are forgiven'.

Perhaps he was aware of something in the man's condition which made his spiritual state of even more pressing concern to him than his immobility. Perhaps there was some psychosomatic element in his paralysis which demanded this approach. But perhaps also Jesus already had an eye not only on the patient himself but also on the scribes in the audience, whose horrified reaction may have been exactly what he aimed to provoke. Their objection, as he must have expected, is not that a declaration of sins is inappropriate to the man's condition, but that it is blasphemous.

## 'Who can forgive?'

Since sin is an offence against God, only God can, in any ultimate sense, forgive it. The scribes' theology was correct, and Jesus does not dispute it. But instead of apologizing or backing off, he defiantly goes on to repeat his outrageous declaration, and even more remarkably, to put his credibility on the line by linking forgiveness with visible healing.

Forgiveness is not a matter of less importance than physical well-being, but it is no doubt easier to *say* 'Your sins are forgiven' than to say to a crippled man, 'Stand up', since the former is not easily verified, while the failure of the man to get up would lay him open to instant ridicule. So by linking the two together Jesus uses his undeniable ability to perform the physical miracle as proof that he also has the authority to perform the greater but less verifiable act of forgiving sin.

## The authority of the Son of man

The issue is one of authority. Jesus claims the right to do what only God can do, and proves it by a spectacular instant healing. The crowd are impressed, while the scribes keep their counsel. But with hindsight we can see here the beginning of the confrontation between this unorthodox and exciting new teacher and the guardians of religious orthodoxy, a confrontation which will develop in the rest of this chapter and into chapter 3 to the point where they begin to plot his overthrow.

The unique authority which he claims is as 'the Son of man', a title used here for the first time in Mark's story, but later to be the basis of some of his most daring claims, and the only title he is willing to adopt publicly. It derives from the great vision of Daniel chapter 7, of 'one like a son of man' who is destined to share the eternal kingship of God himself. Jesus certainly does not suffer from false modesty!

### PRAYER

*Lord Jesus, healer of bodies and of souls, we bring to you ourselves in all our varied needs, and rejoice in your unique authority to meet them.*

# 14 Disreputable company

Tax collectors are probably never popular, but in Roman Palestine their reputation stood at an all-time low. In Galilee they represented Herod Antipas, the unpopular half-Jewish ruler, who in turn represented Roman occupation. So a tax collector was a collaborator, and his association with the pagan occupying power made him religiously as well as politically suspect. Moreover, he was paid no salary, since it was assumed that he would collect more than the amount he was obliged to pass on to his superiors, and would keep the difference; some tax collectors lived very comfortably as a result. So the linking of 'tax collectors and sinners' would come naturally to a Jewish mind. They formed a sort of underclass, ostracized from decent society.

## The call of Levi

Levi is apparently the same person as 'Matthew' in 3:18 (see Matthew 9:9–13, where the same tax collector is called 'Matthew'). In the border town of Capernaum he would probably be employed in collecting customs duties. He is the only disciple whose call is specifically recorded after the initial four fishermen—the inclusion of a tax collector among Jesus' closest associates was remarkable enough to be worth a special mention. Like Peter and his associates, he left his job to be with Jesus; but no doubt his reputation followed him. We can only imagine how the other disciples felt about the inclusion of a tax collector in their select company!

## Tax collectors and sinners

But we do not need to imagine what other people thought, because Mark tells us. The horror of the scribes no doubt reflects the general reaction of polite society. Jesus has carried unconventional behaviour to the point of scandal. It was bad enough for Jesus to call a tax collector to follow him, but when that new disciple gathers a houseful of his associates for a party, and Jesus and his other disciples are seen eating with them, that is too much to bear in silence. For to eat with someone is the ultimate mark of acceptance and identification, and no respectable Jew would be seen eating in such company.

Jesus' response is a classic, and highlights the basic difference between his understanding of his own mission and the scribes' idea of holiness. For them, to please God was to keep yourself as pure as possible, and in practice that was bound to mean limiting the places you went and the company you kept. For Jesus, the priority was not to protect his own personal sanctity but to meet people where they were, and to offer new hope to those whom society had disowned. By comparing himself with a doctor, and the 'sinners' with patients, Jesus distances himself irrevocably from the scribes' concept of the religious life. He has come, as he said later in another tax-collector's house, 'to seek out and to save the lost' (Luke 19:10), and if that means getting his hands dirty, so be it.

## FOR MEDITATION

*Who would be the social equivalent in our society to the tax collectors of Roman Palestine? How does our own attitude to them, and the attitude of the church in general, match up to that of Jesus? How good are we at 'calling sinners'?*

# 15 Old and new in religion

In the Old Testament the annual day of fasting on the Day of Atonement is the only fast laid down for everyone, but it is clear that other fasts were observed by different groups of people, and the Pharisees had by this time developed a much more rigorous scheme involving weekly fasts (see Luke 18:12). John the Baptist was known as an ascetic (1:6; cf. Matthew 11:18), so it is not surprising that his followers had adopted a similar practice. Jesus accepted the value of fasting (Matthew 6:16–18), but did not impose such a scheme on his disciples. So those whose idea of religion focused on self-imposed discipline would naturally see him as less serious in his religious observance, and wanted to know why.

## Feasting and fasting

Jesus' reply suggests that something new and exciting is going on, as far as he and his disciples are concerned. It is like a wedding-feast, a time for celebration not for enforced gloom. The party in Levi's house is more appropriate to the new situation of the coming of the kingdom of God than is the old, tired system of self-discipline practised by the Pharisees.

But along with the celebration goes a note of realism. One day the bridegroom will be taken away from them, and the party will be over. Here is the first indication in Mark's story that Jesus knew all along that there were dark days ahead, and that his ultimate death in Jerusalem would not come as a surprise to him, however little his disciples may have been able to imagine it during these early days of euphoria. At that time fasting will be more appropriate than feasting, though Jesus' allusive words do not add up to a formal régime of fasting for the church to adopt.

## New into old won't go

Two further pictures are used to emphasize how different the new situation is, and how incompatible with the old. A piece of strong new cloth should not be used to patch a worn cloak, since the old cloth does not have the strength to resist the pull of the new. And there is a power in new wine which is too much for old containers to resist, as many home brewers know to their cost, even in these days of glass bottles. The leather wineskins of biblical days soon became brittle with age, and were no match for the pressure of fermentation.

That is what it is like when you try to contain the effervescent life of the kingdom of God within the traditional patterns of Jewish religion. Something has to give. This is, no doubt, a sad comment on the confrontation which is already developing in this chapter between Jesus and the representatives of the old régime. He is too strong for them to take. The new life of the kingdom of God is increasingly demanding, and creating, a new religious structure to contain it.

The truth illustrated by these two vivid pictures applies not only to first-century Judaism, but has been played out again and again in the history of Christianity too. Traditional forms of religion tend to 'dry up', and when new life comes it has to break out. It needs great wisdom to recognize what is good among the new trends of our own times, and to design the right sort of 'wineskins' to contain it.

### PRAYER
*Thank you, Lord Jesus, for the new life you came to bring. Help us not only to enjoy it, but also to channel it in ways which will preserve it intact for those who come after us.*

# 16 In the cornfields

The sabbath was one of the most distinctive features of Judaism, and was guarded with fierce national pride. The Old Testament itself gave little specific guidance as to how it was to be 'kept holy', beyond the general injunction to 'do no work'. But what is work, and are even necessary types of work forbidden? Here was a fertile field for scribal debate and definition, and their rules and regulations, designed to make it easier for people to know when they were and were not breaking the sabbath law, went into ever more meticulous detail. One of their chief complaints against Jesus was that he did not seem to share their enthusiasm for sabbath regulations.

## What was wrong with what the disciples were doing?

Plucking a few ears of grain was not in itself illegal (Deuteronomy 23:25). But among the thirty-nine categories of work which the scribes had identified as forbidden on the sabbath were reaping and threshing, and what they were doing was a sort of reaping (and when you add Luke's comment that they rubbed the ears in their hands, Luke 6:1, it was threshing too!).

Jesus does not dispute that the sabbath day should be kept holy; nor does he enter into discussion of the precise definition of work which the Pharisees are assuming. His response is at the more fundamental level of what the sabbath was for in the first place, and of who has authority to determine how it is observed. He thus undercuts the whole edifice of scribal definitions of 'work' by going back to first principles.

## Jesus and the sabbath

His first argument is that if David could flout the law, so can he! This sounds a pretty thin defence, if all that is being asserted is that if the law has been broken once it can be broken again. But the point is not the mere fact that the law was broken before, but rather who it was who broke it. David could do it because he was David, God's anointed king. He came to the high priest on an urgent mission, and the high priest gave him a special dispensation to make use of the consecrated bread (1 Samuel 21:1–6; this may have been on the sabbath, since that was the day the bread was changed, but that is not the point of Jesus' allusion). The implication is left unspoken, but surely it is that Jesus has a status and authority at least equivalent to that of David.

The second argument builds on this claim to a special authority. It has two parts. First, what is the sabbath for?—not to make life difficult for people, but to be a blessing to them. By hedging it about with regulations the scribes had turned a joyful divine provision into a burden. Secondly, who has the right to interpret the sabbath?— Jesus ('the Son of man') is its 'Lord'. Here again we meet that awesome title from the book of Daniel, which is in itself a claim to share the authority of the God who himself instituted the sabbath. But the literal meaning of 'a son of man' is simply a human being, and so Jesus draws also on the first half of his argument. If the sabbath was made for human beings, who better to pronounce on its proper use than *the* Human Being?

No wonder the Pharisees found Jesus hard to take! Who did he think he was?

## FOR MEDITATION

*In the light of Jesus' arguments here, what should be our priorities with regard to keeping one day in seven as a 'holy' day? Is it important for us to try to determine, for ourselves and for others, what is 'work'? If so, how can this be decided?*

# 17 More trouble on the sabbath

The encounter in the cornfields may have been just a chance meeting which gave rise to an argument. But this time there is certainly nothing accidental about the confrontation in the synagogue. It almost looks as though the man has been 'planted' to provide a test-case. At any rate, the Pharisees are watching Jesus, with a view to finding evidence against him.

## Healing on the sabbath

Healing would normally involve some sort of work (preparing medicine, binding wounds, etc.), and so fell outside the scribes' definition of what could be permitted on the sabbath. The only concession allowed was if there was imminent danger to life, but clearly a 'withered hand' (probably some form of paralysis) could wait until the next day. It might be suggested that the scribal rules would not apply to the sort of healing Jesus normally practised, by a mere word of command, since no 'work' was involved. But a healing was a healing, and the scribal law forbade it. So 'they watched him'.

It looks as though Jesus takes the initiative, since Mark makes no mention of an appeal for help from the man himself. He is aware of what the Pharisees have planned, but he is as eager as they are to get the issue into the open, and decides to take the fight to them. The healing will follow in due course, as authoritatively and immediately as usual, but first the principle of sabbath healing needs to be sorted out.

## A question of priorities

Jesus' question, like his comments in the cornfield, goes to the heart of what the sabbath is all about. These are not the terms in which the scribes were accustomed to debating sabbath issues. They could discuss with great skill what did and did not constitute work, and how in practice life could be allowed to carry on while still keeping the sabbath 'holy'. But to put the issue in terms as broad and as un-legal as simply 'to do good or to do harm, to save life or to kill' was to shift the debate onto uncomfortably far-reaching grounds, for which their detailed debates had not prepared them. So 'they were silent'.

But Jesus has not merely succeeded in silencing his opponents. He has also again given an important clue to how religious rules such as the sabbath law need to be interpreted. Taken together with his pronouncement in 2:27 that the sabbath was made for humankind, and not humankind for the sabbath, this principle of aiming to 'do good' on the sabbath leaves detailed casuistry (trying not to break the rules) behind, and takes us onto the far more demanding ground of positively looking for the way of keeping the sabbath holy which will most benefit one's fellow human beings. If to 'do good' involves setting aside a scribal ruling, then it is the ruling which must go. So Jesus heals the man's hand.

## Mutual rejection

In verse 5, as probably in 1:41, Mark tells us that Jesus was 'angry'. What annoys him this time is clear, the willingness to put the keeping of man-made rules before the well-being of other people. Perhaps also it is the Pharisees' deliberate attempt to incriminate him which annoys him. But they are no less annoyed, partly by his (as they see it) flagrant flouting of the law, and partly by the cavalier way in which he has asserted his general principle of 'goodness' over against their concept of holiness, leaving them silenced and humiliated. The healing in itself may not seem like a capital offence, but the last two encounters have revealed an increasingly unbridgeable gulf between Jesus' understanding of religion and theirs. The man is dangerous, and must be eliminated. It will still take some time, but the wheels are in motion which will ultimately take Jesus to the cross.

### PRAYER

*Help us, Lord Jesus, to see things in your perspective, to put the positive doing of God's will above the mere avoidance of breaking the rules, and so to seek always to 'do good' rather than to keep out of trouble.*

# 18 Beside the seaside

The 'sea', here as elsewhere in Mark's story, is of course the Lake of Galilee, a large fresh-water inland lake, enclosed by hills, and the scene of the thriving fishing industry from which Jesus has already drawn four of his followers. The shore of the lake in the area around Capernaum is the setting for much of the narrative in these early chapters of the Gospel. It was a natural gathering ground, which allowed much larger crowds to gather than was possible in the constricted streets of Capernaum itself.

## Growing popularity

In contrast with the hostility of the religious establishment is the increasing crowd of ordinary people who are now coming to find Jesus. They have come 'hearing all that he was doing', and no doubt it is his miraculous activity as much as his teaching which is drawing them. But as we have already seen in 1:38, Jesus' primary concern is with his teaching mission, and this is what he is doing with the crowds on the lake shore (2:13). The request for a boat is not only to allow him to escape from the physical pressure of the crowds of people clamouring to be healed, but also to provide him with a more detached 'pulpit' from which he will be able to address the crowd as a whole, as we shall see him doing in 4:1-2.

The list of places from which the people have come is interesting. Naturally they are mainly locals from Galilee, but the other areas mentioned extend not only to the rest of the Jewish territory (Judea, Jerusalem, and across the Jordan), but also to the related but distinct people of Idumea (Edom of the Old Testament), and to the more thoroughly non-Jewish people of Tyre and Sidon. These are among the traditional enemies of Israel, and their people would not be seen as fit company for a pious Jew. While Mark will not say much about Jesus' activity among non-Jews until later in his Gospel, already we can see that the Messiah of Israel is happy to extend his mission more broadly, and that among some of those who could not claim to belong to the 'chosen people' he meets with a better response than he has found among the leaders of the Jews.

## Healing and exorcism

As before (1:32, 34) a clear distinction is made between the cure of diseases and the conflict with unclean spirits. But in both areas Jesus' power is extraordinary. A mere touch seems to be enough to secure physical healing, while demonic forces spontaneously recognize his superior authority. This recognition of Jesus by supernatural beings is clearly important to Mark (1:24, 34; cf. 5:7). It is the reluctant testimony of those who have more than human insight that in Jesus they are confronted by a new and altogether overwhelming spiritual power. Such testimony to the uniqueness of Jesus, despite the unwholesome source from which it comes, is real evidence that Jesus truly is the Son of God, and confirms the declaration already made by God himself (1:11).

But, important as this testimony is now for Mark's readers, at the time Jesus did not welcome it, and again we hear the command to silence. Jesus prefers as yet to remain incognito, however great his popular following. The time to declare the full extent of his authority as the Son of God has not yet come; it will ring out with full clarity only in 14:61–62, and by that time it will be too late for people to misunderstand the nature of his mission and to try to divert him into a less spiritual role.

**PRAYER**

*Thank you, Lord Jesus, that you welcome people from any background, and that you meet their needs. May we come to you and find not only the help we want, but also the help we need.*

# 19

# Twelve good men
# and true?

This was an important moment, the selection, from among the many people who were following Jesus, of the task force on whom the extension of his mission would depend, not only while he himself was still there to supervise them (6:7–13, 30–31) but more importantly after he was gone. This is the foundation on which the Christian church was to be built.

## A firm foundation?

Simon, natural leader as he was in many ways, was one day to disown his Lord. James and John, whose nickname suggests at least an unhealthy degree of self-confidence, would need to be publicly humiliated for their crass misunderstanding of Jesus' mission (10:35–45). Most of the others are little more than names to us; they do not seem to have left much of a mark in history. They include one odd combination: Matthew, if he is the same as Levi (2:14), was one whose profession was anathema to patriotic Jews, while the other Simon was a 'Cananaean', the Aramaic term for a zealot, a political activist dedicated to the liberation of his people from the very régime which employed Matthew! And then, appropriately listed right at the end, there is Judas, whose notorious story is laconically indicated by the words 'who betrayed him'.

Not a very inspired choice? But God has always been ready to work through fallible human sources, and to put his treasure in earthen vessels. No doubt most of us, using proper screening and management criteria, could have done a better job. But as God warned Samuel, 'the Lord does not see as mortals see'. So perhaps there is hope for the rest of us after all!

Nowadays such a shortlist might have led to prosecution under sex discrimination legislation. In the social and cultural situation of the time, however, the inclusion of women in this particular task force would have been a quick route to scandal and to the unthinking rejection of Jesus' mission before it had begun, quite apart from the practical problems of a mixed group sharing the conditions of Jesus' itinerant ministry.

## The job description

'Apostle' means 'sent', and these twelve men are indeed to be sent out to share in the activities for which Jesus himself has already become famous. They too will proclaim the same message; they too will have authority to cast out demons. It is an awesome responsibility, and one for which this motley group may well have felt ill-equipped. But that is only the second part of their job description. First comes the element on which all the rest depends, 'to be with him'.

They will be with him in the very basic sense that from now on Jesus will be accompanied by this group wherever he goes (except on a few occasions when he will take only the core group of Peter, James and John). They will travel, eat and sleep together, sharing his itinerant existence and his dependence on the hospitality and the gifts of well-wishers. But they will be with him also in the deeper sense that increasingly as time goes on he will devote himself to training and instructing them, rebuking their clumsiness, correcting their misunderstandings, patiently preparing them for the role of leadership which they will too soon have to assume. It is only because they have been 'with him' that they will be up to the task.

**FOR MEDITATION**
*What are the criteria for responsibility and leadership among the followers of Jesus? What have we, and what has the church today, to learn from the way Jesus selected and trained his task force?*

# 20 How do you explain Jesus?

Mark sometimes likes to enfold one story within another (or to 'sandwich' it) so as to help his readers to listen to the one in the light of the other. He has done that in the latter part of chapter 3. Within the story of how Jesus' own family responded to his extraordinary behaviour (3:20–21, 31–35) he has enclosed an altogether more hostile and threatening encounter with some scribes from Jerusalem. What the two stories have in common is that each group is struggling to find ways of making sense of Jesus. They have heard about his remarkable activity, especially about his exorcisms, and, since they cannot simply dismiss the stories as untrue, they need an explanation. Yet neither group yet believes his claim to be working by the power of God. The alternative explanations they come up with are not very flattering: his family think he is mad, and the scribes accuse him of being in league with the devil!

## Familiarity breeds contempt

Most of us must have some sympathy with Jesus' mother and brothers and sisters. To have a member of the family behave in such an unconventional way, and become a public spectacle, is deeply embarrassing. Unlike the thronging crowds, they cannot believe that someone they have known all his life can be that special. He is making a fool of himself, and, for his own good, he must be stopped. (Incidentally, where NRSV has 'people were saying', the Greek is simply '*they* were saying', and the 'they' reads most naturally as the family themselves.)

In verse 21 they set out on this mission, and in verse 31 they will arrive. We shall see then how Jesus responds to their well-meaning scepticism.

# In league with Beelzebul

Mark makes a point of the fact that the scribes are not locals (like those of 2:6, 16, 24; 3:6). Now there is an even more threatening note: scribes have come into Galilee from the capital, Jerusalem, to question his activity. We shall meet more scribes from Jerusalem in 7:1, again coming up to Galilee and making trouble for Jesus. These are strong hints of the confrontation which is to come when Jesus eventually leaves Galilee for Jerusalem.

Their accusation is altogether more damaging than the scepticism of Jesus' family, and will sting Jesus into a much more scathing reply. Beelzebul was a popular name for Satan, the chief of the demons. To accuse Jesus of complicity with Beelzebul was to imply that he practised black magic, or worse. Even more than that, the phrase 'He has Beelzebul' probably means also that he is himself possessed by an evil spirit, indeed by the most evil of all. That is how Mark will interpret their accusation in verse 30. So, far from being the deliverer of those in the grip of spiritual evil, he is himself under its control, and his supposed exorcisms are in fact forwarding the purposes of Satan, not defeating them.

In verses 23–30 we will hear Jesus' response to this scandalous accusation. Then in verses 31–35 we will return to the family. The two groups, in contrast with the eager crowds and the committed disciples, represent the failure of some to grasp the significance of what was happening in the ministry of Jesus, and their defensive reaction is that of people who are out of their depth. People can still today be polarized by their responses to Jesus. It is hard to be indifferent about him.

## PRAYER

*Help us, O God, so to grasp the truth about Jesus that we may respond rightly to his challenge, and not resort to contrived explanations, however well-meant, which weaken or deny that truth.*

# 21 'Blasphemy against the Holy Spirit'

## For Satan or against him?

In verses 23–27 Jesus offers what might be called a 'common-sense' reply. The scribes' accusation does not make sense. Why should Satan want Jesus to drive out his own demonic forces. That would be to divide and weaken his own power. The sensible interpretation of the exorcisms (whose reality the scribes clearly cannot deny) is that it is a successful assault on Satan (the 'strong man'), not an act of homage to him!

Jesus is the plunderer of the 'strong man's' house, and the fact that he can do so shows that Satan is powerless ('tied up') before him. The conflict which was foreshadowed in 1:12–13 has now been well and truly joined, and Jesus is proving himself the stronger. The kingdom of Satan is giving way before the kingdom of God.

## The unforgivable sin

But Jesus does not leave his response at that level of 'sensible' argument. This is more than a polite academic debate. He confronts these scornful scribes with one of the most severe warnings in the Bible. They are in danger of committing, indeed may already have committed, the unforgivable sin.

There is an amazing breadth to verse 28—*any* sin or blasphemy may be forgiven. But to appeal to it as a sort of *carte blanche* is to take it out of context, for its function here is to place in stark contrast the one sin which is declared to be beyond the scope of forgiveness, that of blasphemy against the Holy Spirit.

This saying has caused untold agony to many who have tortured themselves with the fear that they too may have committed the unforgivable sin. In most cases that fear is quite groundless. It derives from the failure to read the text in its context. And Mark has gone out of his way to help us to interpret it correctly, since he adds his own explanatory comment, '—for they had said, "He has an unclean spirit"'. He could hardly be more explicit. This is not a vague, general threat to anyone who may have had unholy thoughts. It is directed against the specific charge of the scribes that Jesus was working by the power of Beelzebul. In so accusing him they were attributing the glorious and manifest work of God to the power of evil, and such a radical perversion of the truth reveals a deliberate hostility against God himself. It is such settled opposition to the work of the divine spirit which Jesus pronounces unforgivable.

This is a far cry from the impure thoughts and words with the memory of which some sensitive souls have tortured themselves. Such people would be better advised to focus their attention on verse 28 rather than on verse 29!

### PRAYER

*Lord, teach us to follow you in all sincerity and truth, and so assure us of the free forgiveness which is your gracious provision in Christ for all who sin and repent.*

# 22 Insiders and outsiders

Here is the other end of the 'sandwich' which began in verses 20–21; the family have arrived. At the same time, a further layer is added to the sandwich, in that the inner circle of the disciples, whose call was narrated just before the family were introduced, now return to the scene, and in this final tableau of chapter three the two groups are memorably placed in contrast. Mark thus wraps up a comprehensive portrayal of the differing levels of response to Jesus: outright hostility (the scribes), well-meaning scepticism (the family) and enthusiastic commitment (the disciples).

## Standing outside

The tableau is carefully constructed. Jesus is in the house, with a crowd of people sitting around him ('in a circle', says the Greek text in verse 34). Here is the group of those who belong. But outside the house, trying to contact Jesus but separated from him, are his family. They do not belong to the group of 'insiders'. The word 'outside' is repeated twice, and in the next chapter the same term will be used with great effect in 4:11 to describe those who are unable to comprehend the secret of the kingdom of God. The family, at this point, remain 'outsiders'.

Mark will tell us no more about Jesus' family in his Gospel, though we know from elsewhere in the New Testament and in early Christian records that eventually most if not all of them became members of the Christian movement, and Jesus' brother James even became the leader of the Jerusalem church. But so far they have not been able to overcome the problem of familiarity and to see Jesus as he really is. And so they provide the basis for a striking, almost shocking, pronouncement by Jesus in verses 33 to 35.

## The true family

Family love and loyalty were as important in Jewish culture as in any other, and the Old Testament insisted strongly on the honour and responsibility which were due between members of the same family. In 7:9–13 we shall hear Jesus rebuking the scribes for trying to erode that honour. And yet here he seems to treat his own family with scant respect, and to claim a closer link with relative strangers than with them.

The links are of a different kind. It is a matter of priority. Jesus has come to call people into the kingdom of God, and those sitting around him in a circle are those who, as far as they are able, have already committed themselves to obey his call. In responding to his teaching they are 'doing the will of God', and that is what matters most of all. As long as Jesus' family are unable to join that movement, the blood relationship must take second place to the new family which is coming into being through Jesus' ministry.

Jesus will teach his disciples later what the cost of true discipleship may be. It is taking up one's cross, and losing one's life. Such a total commitment to the kingdom of God will inevitably produce tension with other loyalties, even so sacred a loyalty as that of the family.

So there is pain implicit in this vivid scene. But there is also splendour, the unheard-of privilege of those who 'do the will of God' that they are called Jesus' brother and sister and mother. In belonging to that new family, they find new worth, new identity, and a whole new range of brothers and sisters who are committed with them to follow Jesus in the great adventure of the kingdom of God.

## FOR MEDITATION

*Is the tension between the two 'families' a significant factor in our discipleship? What are the practical implications of this tension in our own situations? And how real for us is the privilege of belonging to a new family with all who 'do the will of God'?*

# 23 Introducing Mark's chapter of parables

In the middle of both the first and third acts of Mark's drama (see study 2 for the three acts) we find what seems like an interlude, where we are offered a concentrated collection of Jesus' teaching before the story resumes at its previous breathless pace. In chapter 13 the teaching will be about what is to happen in the future. Here in chapter 4 we will hear Jesus teaching in parables, and will be invited to think about how the 'secret of the kingdom of God' is both revealed and kept secret.

Perhaps Mark as a story-teller feels the need to allow his readers a pause in the action in order to take stock. But in this chapter we are doing much more than marking time. For the conflicts and divisions we have seen in chapters 2 and 3 have raised important questions, and it is time for those questions to be faced directly.

## What has happened to the 'kingdom of God'?

The fanfare with which Jesus' public ministry began in 1:14–15 left the reader expecting dramatic developments as the newly-declared kingship of God began to be implemented. And sure enough there have been spectacular healings and exorcisms, enthusiastic crowds, and the gathering of a committed group of companions to share Jesus' mission. But it has all been at a limited local level, around the small country towns and villages of Galilee, and among the sort of people who do not usually produce the opinion-formers of society.

And, worse, along with the enthusiasts we have seen sceptics and outright opponents of this new movement. The forces of opposition are gathering, particularly among those who hold real power in the region, and the outlook is increasingly ominous. And even among the crowds who are following Jesus, there is the suspicion that their interest is more in miracles and healing than in the coming of the kingdom of God. How long will their enthusiasm last?

All this is deeply perplexing for those who have understood the revolutionary implications of Jesus' announcement of the kingdom of God. How can God's purpose be resisted? How can so dynamic a message meet with such a mixed response? Does this really look like the 'fulfilment of the time' (1:15)?

## Teaching in parables

It is with just these questions that the parables of chapter 4 are concerned. They invite us to question our natural assumptions about how God will fulfil his purpose in the world, and offer us a new perspective. And they lay firmly upon us, as upon those who heard Jesus' teaching at the time, the responsibility to examine our own grasp of the divine purpose, and our own response to the searching message of Jesus.

There are in this chapter three 'story-parables' of the sort which the term 'parable' most naturally suggests to the modern reader (4:3–8, 26–29, 30–32). All of them are drawn from agriculture, and all compare the preaching of the kingdom of God with the sowing of seed. But these three little stories are only a part of the rich mixture of pictorial teaching and explanatory comments which this chapter offers, and all of these too are included in the summary statement that 'with many such parables he spoke the word to them' (v. 33). So before we start to look at the parables individually it will be worth our while in the next study to think a bit more about what parables are, and how they work.

**PRAYER**

*Help us to accept, Lord, that your way of doing things is not always what we would expect, and to be ready to learn to see things, as far as we may, from your point of view.*

51

# 24 What is a parable?

In 3:23 Mark said that Jesus was speaking 'in parables'. But he was not there telling stories of the sort the word 'parable' suggests to us. The Greek word *parabole* is in fact a more general term which includes also riddles, puzzles, epigrams (as in 7:15), and other forms of vivid teaching. A *parabole* is a striking pronouncement, short or long, which leaves the hearers to work out for themselves what it was all about. It is likely to leave them stimulated, exhilarated, challenged, perhaps puzzled, but it will not spoonfeed them with a simple prosaic statement.

And this means that the same parable may have a very different effect on different people. One may be left puzzled or indifferent, while another sees a flash of light and will never be the same again. One may go away bored, while another will be decisively set on a new course of life. One may say politely 'What an interesting story', while another will exclaim, 'Yes, of course, I see it all now'. Parables, by their very nature, divide people, because each individual will respond to them differently.

## Parables and cartoons

Parables have been helpfully compared with political cartoons in a newspaper. The cartoonist's picture, often without any words, carries a profound comment on current affairs, and at its best may shock a reader into a new assessment of events or even a new political allegiance. But how much you get out of the cartoon depends on how much you bring to it, in terms of your knowledge of what is going on in the world, and your awareness of the conventions of cartoon-drawing, as well as sharpness of mind, openness to new ideas, and a willingness to think through the implications with the cartoonist.

Parables, like cartoons, will affect different people in different ways, and those who benefit from them will be those who come with a mind prepared. Some will prove to have what it takes; others will not. As we read through this chapter we shall see that this is precisely why they formed such an suitable vehicle for Jesus' teaching in the situation of mixed responses to the preaching of the kingdom of God which chapters 2–3 have described.

## Setting the scene

Jesus is back beside the lake, and again the boat is on hand to give him a detached 'pulpit' from which he can speak more easily to the large number of people. Such a large crowd will have within it people in many different states of readiness and ability to grasp what he has to say. How can so mixed an audience be effectively taught all at once? Surely through stories and pictures, and in such teaching Jesus is the expert. So they, and we, will now hear 'many things in parables'.

### FOR MEDITATION

*Jesus is sometimes described as the greatest teacher the world has known. Mark tells us that his typical method of teaching was in parables. What does this have to say to us about the sort of teaching which really communicates, and about what the aim of that teaching should be? How can we learn from Jesus' teaching method in our own attempts to communicate divine truth?*

# 25 What happened to the seeds?

The Parable of the Sower draws on the familiar experiences of a Palestinian farmer, even if not every farmer was so unlucky as to have all these types of problem ground on his farm at once. Jesus is not inventing a fantasy scenario, but using common everyday experience to illustrate the coming of the kingdom of God.

## The seeds that failed

In well-ploughed ground much of the seed would fall immediately out of sight, and could quickly take root. But where a path had been trodden across the field there was nowhere for the seed to hide, and no soft earth for the roots to penetrate. It was fair game for the birds.

In most of Galilee the rock is close to the surface, so that what appears to be good soil proves too shallow to support roots or to retain moisture. The seed could start to grow, but it would not last long in a hot climate. What looked so promising at first would soon be withered.

Even where the soil was deep enough, it might not be unoccupied. Remember our cornfields before selective weedkillers? A well-established growth of weeds was bound to win in the end.

## The seeds that succeeded

Translations usually obscure the fact that whereas the first three seeds are each described in the singular, in verse 8 we change to the plural: 'other seeds fell into good soil...', after which *three* levels of yield are mentioned. So Mark seems to want us to picture *six* seeds, three which failed and three which succeeded, but to varying degrees.

Commentators argue whether yields of 30, 60 and 100 are just good or totally exceptional and miraculous. It depends whether you are reckoning grains per plant, grains per seed sown, or what. But

Genesis 26:12 suggests that we are not here in the realm of fantasy, but of very good crops under the blessing of God.

## If you have ears, listen

We shall hear an 'official' explanation of the parable in verses 14–20, and will think more then about why Jesus told the story like this. The careful spelling out of the fate of the individual seeds suggests that he was concerned with more than just the promise that after all the disappointments there will be a good harvest in the end. We are meant to think about the reasons why the first three seeds failed. They will help to explain why the response to the preaching of the kingdom of God has proved to be so varied. It is not that there is anything wrong with the seed, but that those who receive it are already conditioned in different ways. Some are quite unreceptive, others superficial, others preoccupied; and even among those who prove receptive, there are different levels of effectiveness in their response to the message.

### FOR MEDITATION

*What do you think those who first heard this parable would have made of it, given the situation which we have seen in chapters 2 and 3? Would it mean the same thing to the crowds and to the disciples? How would it affect both their understanding of what was happening and their personal response? And are those lessons relevant to us in our different situation? If so, how?*

# 26

# The secret

These three verses go to the heart of the problem of the divided response to Jesus and his message. They raise acutely the problem of why, when the same gospel is preached, some believe and others do not. But it is another matter how far they offer an answer!

## Explaining the parables

Even the twelve (and the wider group of supporters indicated by 'those who were around him') did not immediately see the point, and had to ask for an explanation. And they will be given an explanation (vv. 14–20). But this will not be in public, but rather 'when he was alone [with them]'. So, as Mark will explain more directly in verses 33–34, there is a division among those who hear Jesus' teaching. For some there is only the parable, and they are apparently unable to understand it without further help. For others there is also the explanation.

So what makes the difference? It is surely significant that those who receive the explanation are those who ask for it. We do not know how wide a circle is represented by 'those who were around him', but they are contrasted with the rest of the crowd, who apparently cannot be bothered to pursue the matter any further. It is those who go on to ask for help who now constitute the 'insiders' as opposed to 'those outside', for whom 'everything comes in parables'—and *only* in parables. Remember the striking double use of 'outside' in 3:31, 32 to contrast Jesus' family with the 'circle' around Jesus. It seems now that the family are only part of a wider group of 'outsiders'.

## The secret of the kingdom of God

Secrecy has been a theme of several of the preceding stories, where Jesus ordered people, and especially demons with their supernatural knowledge, not to talk about who he was and what he was doing. This is reserved information, a 'secret' kept for some and not for others. The ability to grasp the significance of the coming of the kingdom of God, and to discern its powerful presence where others can see only a small group of itinerant peasants, is not for everyone. That, after all, is what the parable of the sower has just illustrated—much of the soil is not capable of producing a crop.

## A depressing precedent

Verse 12 is an abbreviated quotation from Isaiah 6:9–10. After his overwhelming vision in the temple Isaiah was sent to proclaim God's message to his people with the warning that they would not listen, indeed that they were incapable of it. That same incomprehension now faces Jesus in at least part of his audience, and prevents their responding and being saved. The situation is nothing new—indeed the only contrast with Isaiah's experience is that whereas his failure was apparently to be total, in Jesus' case at least there are some to whom the secret is revealed.

The worst bit of verse 12 is the conjunction with which it begins: 'in order that' suggests that God and/or Jesus *wants* the message to fail. But it is too literalistic to read this as meaning that God is deliberately keeping people out of his kingdom. The point is rather that they are already by their own nature outsiders, and that teaching in parables merely brings out into the open the division which is already there. The sowing of the seed does not ruin the soil—it is rather the condition of the soil which determines the fate of the seed.

But if this passage does not declare God's determination to keep people out of the kingdom of God, neither does it explain how outsiders can become insiders. The disciples to whom the secret has been revealed were once themselves outsiders. How they have made the transition is a question which must be answered from elsewhere, unless it be by the observation that it is they, and not the outsiders, who have come asking questions.

### PRAYER

*When we are confronted by mysteries, O God, help us earnestly to seek the answers from you, and to rejoice in what has been revealed, but also to accept that we may not yet be able to understand all your truth.*

# 27
# Spelling it out

Mark will tell us in verse 34 that Jesus explained everything in private to his disciples. In that case, this detailed spelling out of what the imagery of the parable represented must be typical of many other such explanations; but this is the only one Mark has recorded for us. It consists of a sort of 'glossary' of what each scene in the story represents, but still leaves it to us to work out what was the point of telling the story, and what his hearers were intended to do about it. 'Let anyone with ears to hear listen'!

## A parable about parables

Verse 13 suggests that to understand this one parable about the sower is the key to understanding other parables too. The intervening verses (10–12) have focused on the divided response which parables, by their very nature, produce, leaving some enlightened and others none the wiser. The parable of the sower, as it is now explained, is precisely about different ways of responding to the message, and shows that some are fruitful soil and some unfruitful. Moreover, it spells out three different types of unproductiveness. All this reinforces the point that the effect of parables depends not only on the message (the seed) being good, but also on the hearers (the soil) being in a condition to receive it. To have understood this is to be on the way to understand how all parables will work, and thus to be alert to the factors in our own and other people's situation which will determine whether the seed can germinate and grow. Those who have ears will hear.

## So what does it mean?

It is natural to want to know 'the answer', to have it spelled out in a single, clear moral which all good hearers can put into practice. But parables are, in their very nature, open-ended. The implications of the truths illustrated in the parable of the sower may be different for different people.

Some may come to it as preachers, puzzled and disappointed that the message of the gospel has met with such a mixed response. Probably their situation is close to that of the original disciples, perplexed by the apparently sporadic progress of the kingdom of God. For them the parable conveys both an explanation of why some are so unresponsive, and the encouragement of knowing that along with the bad soil there is also the good, that after the waste there will be the harvest.

Others may need to be challenged as to their own openness to the call of God. For them the call is to examine themselves against the different types of unfruitful ground, and to take steps to improve the condition of their own soil.

Some, while not unfruitful, may be only too aware that the best they can do produces only quite a modest result, while others seem to be spectacularly effective as disciples. For them it is important to realize that within the purpose of God not all good soil is in the hundredfold bracket.

There are, no doubt, many other appropriate ways of reading the story and its explanation. Jesus has given us the template. It is for each of us to fit it to our own situation and questions. Even for the same reader the parable's message and challenge may not always be the same. That is how parables work.

## FOR MEDITATION

*What does the parable of the sower mean for you?*

28
# More pregnant sayings

*MARK 4:21-25*

Before we come to the two other 'story-parables' of chapter 4, Mark offers us a collection of short sayings which together explore further the nature of revelation and how we must respond to the truth revealed. The language, while full of vivid imagery, is rather mysterious, and the implications of the sayings are not clearly spelled out. The reader is again left to think it out and to come to his or her own conclusions. In other words, we are here, just as much as in the stories about seed, in the realm of parable.

## Let the light shine

The picture in verse 21 is clear enough: a lamp is no use if it is hidden away; it needs to be put where its light can be most effectively seen. So hidden things must be disclosed. Secrets are meant to be divulged (v. 22).

But what does this mean? Is it an exhortation by Jesus to his disciples to share with others the special understanding of the kingdom of God which they have received (v. 11)? But in that case how does it relate to the theme of secrecy which is so prominent in Mark's Gospel, and especially to the assumption of verses 11–12 (and indeed of the parable of the sower) that there are some who will not be able to see the light, and that Jesus teaches in parables for just this reason? If everything is to be made plain, why does he himself not use a less ambiguous form of teaching? Perhaps we are to read these verses as a deliberate counterweight to the apparent exclusivism of verses 11–12. God's ultimate purpose is not concealment but enlightenment.

Or are these verses a promise to the disciples that what at present is still under wraps will one day be brought into the open? Despite the declaration of verse 11, their own understanding is still far from complete, and they must wait with patience for further light to dawn.

As in verse 9, the parable formula ('Let anyone with ears to hear listen') again challenges the reader to think through what these enigmatic words might mean in practice.

# Listen with care

The basic principle of verses 24–25 is that what you get out depends on what you put in. We have seen already that this is in the nature of parables. Those who come to them with the right background and the right attitude will find them a source of further enlightenment. Those who come with nothing will take away nothing. Indeed, as in capitalist economics, the inequality tends to be compounded rather than corrected. Those who give good measure will receive back not only what they brought, but more as well, while those who start with nothing will finish up with, if possible, even less!

This principle, when applied to the hearing of parables, chimes in with the parable of the sower. The seed which is not well received is lost or withered, while that which finds a good response will grow and multiply. The same message can be received effectually and ineffectually. So be careful how you hear, and don't let the message go in through one ear and out of the other.

There is a tension between verses 21–22, with their apparently optimistic expectation that what is hidden will be revealed, and verses 24–25, which reinforce the message of the first part of the chapter that not all who hear will be enlightened. These verses do not offer a simple 'theology of revelation'. But they do offer a clear challenge to the reader to be sure to finish up on the right side of the divide.


**PRAYER**

*Lord, save us from carelessness over your truth. Make us good hearers, and doers of what we hear. And use us to bring to light for others what at present is hidden from them.*

# 29

# The dynamics of growth

This time we are offered no explanation, beyond the opening phrase, 'The kingdom of God is as if...' Or, to paraphrase it, 'This is how God works out his purpose in the world'. For 'the kingdom of God', remember, means God being king, God in his sovereign power, God taking control. So 'the kingdom of God' is not something which we can achieve, or even promote. It is what God does. And that, of course, is just what this little parable is about.

## Watching the seed grow

The account of arable farming given in this parable is simplified almost to the point of caricature. The farmer sows the seed, and then has nothing more to do until he comes back to gather the harvest. Would that it were so easy! What about ploughing and harrowing, fertilizers and weedkillers, drought and storms, birds and vermin? But of course this is not meant to be a guide to arable farming. It is a picture, simply drawn, to help us understand how God works in his world.

The focus is on the dynamic of growth which the seed has in itself. The farmer knows it will happen, but he neither causes it nor can he explain it. The power of growth is, as it were, built into the seed. So the ground, once it has received the seed, cannot help producing a crop (forget now about the parable of the sower; this is a different parable!). The process is, to use the Greek word at the beginning of verse 28, 'automatic', both in the beginning of the seed's growth and in the predetermined stages through which it passes from the initial shoot to the 'full grain in the head'.

## God's initiative

To the disciples, puzzled by the fact that Jesus' powerful proclamation of the kingdom of God does not yet seem to have had the desired effect, the story suggests that they may wait with patient confidence, for the seed is sown and it is sure to grow. But it will grow in God's way and in God's time, and can neither be hindered nor hurried.

The moral might seem to be that the proper attitude is one of laid-back optimism with a minimum of effort. Just leave it all to God, and the harvest will be there in the end. If this parable stood alone that might seem a plausible interpretation. But the same Jesus who told it will later send his disciples out with a sense of urgency to summon people to respond to the announcement of the kingdom of God (6:7–12)—as indeed he himself has been doing with a similar sense of urgency (1:38–39).

The point seems rather to be that we should not make the mistake of imagining that we can take over God's work and make him effectively irrelevant. The proclamation is of *God's* kingship. His subjects undoubtedly have a vital role to play in disseminating it, but it is his power, not theirs, which will bring it to fruition. This is the basis for due humility on the part of his disciples, but also for unshakeable confidence that the promised harvest really will come, because it is God himself who will produce it.

## PRAYER

*Thank you, Lord, that your kingdom is established by your own power, not by our ability. Help us to cooperate in your sovereign work, and to have full confidence that in our day, as in the days of Jesus, you will produce the harvest.*

# 30

# From the least to the greatest

## Mustard seed

Mustard seed is proverbially tiny (see Matthew 17:20), and yet it produces 'the greatest of all shrubs'. This is not, of course, the puny 'mustard-and-cress' that we grow in little plastic boxes, but a garden herb which in Palestine commonly grew to a height of three metres. Such a spectacular result from such an unpromising beginning is the stuff of which proverbs are made ('Great oaks from little acorns grow'), and provides Jesus with a clear and compelling illustration for what the kingdom of God is like (see the previous study for what this means). Its beginnings may be unimpressive, even virtually invisible—but just you wait and see!

Both supporters and sceptics may have found it hard to see the powerful inbreaking of the kingdom of God in this motley group of villagers trudging around the countryside with their eccentric leader. They were far from the corridors of power. Could such a movement change the world? Looking back, we know the answer, and Jesus' parable warns them not to 'despise the day of small things' (Zechariah 4:10). There is a pervasive sense of the incognito about Jesus' ministry as Mark records it, and he makes no secret of the fact that many (most?) failed to grasp the significance of what was going on in their neighbourhood. For the disciples, who were at least beginning to grasp it, the need was for patience. God's purpose will be worked out in his own time and way. The seed *will* grow, for that is the nature of seed—and of the kingdom of God.

## Rounding it off

Verses 33–34 round off the whole collection of Jesus' teaching in parables by reiterating the pattern we have already seen repeatedly through this chapter. Parables are for everyone; explanations are only for the disciples, in private. This sounds like a device for maintaining the 'secret of the kingdom of God' by keeping the truth away from the wider crowds. It almost sounds as though Jesus doesn't want the people in general to understand.

But Mark adds the interesting rider 'as they were able to hear it'. We are reminded again of the parable of the sower—the effectiveness of the seed depends on how far people are 'able to hear'. As Jesus speaks in parables, there are some who will simply not see the point, and will enquire no further. These are the people for whom 'everything comes in parables' (v. 11), and who will receive no explanation. But if we were right in suggesting that 'those who were around him' (v. 10) includes not only the already committed disciples but others who, as a result of hearing the parables, want to know more, it may be that such people too are now among the 'disciples' for whom explanations are said to be available in verse 34.

## FOR MEDITATION

*Are we too ready to jump to superficial conclusions about the work of God, or to try to hurry him on? Can you identify places where God is quietly and secretly at work in your own context?*

*How can we best present the message of Jesus 'as people are able to hear'? Does Jesus' pattern of teaching by parable and (private) explanation offer us an appropriate model for our day?*

# 31
# Storm at sea

In 1986 the complete hull of a cedar-wood fishing boat from about the first century AD was discovered buried in the mud by the shore of the Lake of Galilee. It is probably typical of the boats in use in Jesus' time. It is just over 8 metres long by 2.35 metres wide and is quite shallow (1.25 metres in depth); there is a slightly raised area at one end. A dozen or so men would fit into it with not much room to spare. To see that boat, in the kibbutz at Ginosar, is to gain a vivid insight into the several stories which Mark tells which are set on or beside the lake. Such a boat would not be a comfortable place to be in a storm.

## What happened on the lake?

The squall was violent enough to scare seasoned fishermen into thoughts of drowning, and yet Jesus was 'asleep on the cushion' (on the raised section at the end of the boat?)! Mark has no inhibitions about portraying Jesus, the Son of God, as also fully human, in his emotions and, as here, in his physical needs. He was apparently exhausted. The disciples' reaction is an intriguing mixture: they clearly expect him to be able to do something about their danger, and yet in their panic wake him with a lack of ceremony which is hardly the way to treat a divine visitor.

Jesus' response is immediate and awesome in its simplicity. A word is enough. He speaks to the wind and waves as if they were living things, rebukes them for their insolence, and dismisses them with a peremptory 'Shut up' (the same vivid expression as he used with the unclean spirit in 1:25). Then he turns on the disciples, and they too suffer a rebuke, though a more gentle one. Didn't they realize whom they had on board with them? Have they learned nothing yet from being with Jesus and from seeing his power? True, all his miracles which Mark has recorded so far relate to people (and the demons who have controlled them), rather than to the forces of nature. But surely they could have put two and two together.

# What did the disciples learn about Jesus?

The disciples are committed to following Jesus, but as yet have had only veiled indications of just who he is (unless they have been able to hear the testimony of the demons before they were silenced, 3:11). They know that he has amazing powers, but to see him controlling even the wind and sea has added a new dimension to their amazement. Many passages in the Old Testament declare that God alone has the power to control the elements (Job 38:8–11; Psalm 107:23–32, etc.), and now here is Jesus enacting those passages in his own right. This is one more vital new step along the road to grasping the full truth about Jesus (which we, the readers, have been privileged to know ever since the opening verses of the Gospel!).

In the mean time, however limited their theological understanding, they are discovering in practice that to follow Jesus is to enter a new realm of possibilities. With Jesus in the boat, what is there to fear?

## PRAYER

*Lord Jesus, help us to discover for ourselves who you are, not only in our minds but also in practical trust and confidence.*

# 32

# A hopeless case

The other (eastern) side of the Lake of Galilee was a very different area, less well-populated, and predominantly non-Jewish (hence the presence of a herd of pigs). Mark does not tell us what purpose Jesus may have had in taking his disciples into this unfamiliar territory, and in moving (for the first but not the last time) outside Jewish society. Perhaps the idea, as in 6:31, was to secure a time of rest after much public activity. The area where Jesus and his disciples landed was apparently some way from any village, and had been taken over by an extraordinarily violent and disturbed man.

## 'We are many'

Mark indulges his story-telling enthusiasm to the full in describing this wretched creature. His threatening behaviour had made him a social outcast, and he had found a home among the tombs, a suitably macabre setting for a man whose life had become a living death.

But his problem is not traced to mental abnormality, but to an outside influence. He is demon-possessed. The 'unclean spirit' to which his condition is attributed in verse 2 has in verse 9 become a whole army of spirits (a 'legion' properly consisted of 6,000 men), and when they are expelled there are apparently enough of them to take over a herd of two thousand pigs. Not that we are obliged to calculate simply on one spirit per pig, but the destruction of such a large herd must indicate an extraordinarily powerful demonic force.

It is useless to speculate how the man's condition might have been diagnosed in our own society with its reluctance to admit anything other than physical and human causes. As far as Mark is concerned, this is the most spectacular manifestation of spiritual evil with which Jesus has yet been confronted, and his confident authority over even so powerful a force of evil brings to a climax the remarkable series of encounters with unclean spirits which have formed so prominent a feature of these early chapters of Mark's Gospel.

# 'Son of the Most High God'

As we have already seen in other such encounters (1:24, 34; 3:11), evil spirits immediately recognize who it is who is now confronting them, and know that their time is up. The terror of the neighbourhood becomes an abject suppliant, as the resident demons beg not to be tormented, and, knowing that they cannot now stay in their 'host', try to negotiate the best terms for withdrawal. The pigs (unclean animals for unclean spirits) are the unfortunate losers in this bizarre piece of bargaining.

For the possessed man it is an amazing deliverance, for Jesus a great victory, for the disciples a spectacular lesson on the authority of their master. The questions which naturally rise in our minds about the apparently cruel fate of the pigs, and the economic loss to their owners, do not seem to trouble Mark at all. No doubt he lived in a less sensitive age, and perhaps he was right not to complicate his story with secondary issues, but modern readers do not find it so easy to pass over such questions (and would not be likely to be helped by the commentator who moralizes on verse 17: 'All down the ages the world has been refusing Jesus because it prefers its pigs'!).

## FOR MEDITATION

*Jesus! the name high over all,*
*In hell or earth or sky;*
*Angels and men before it fall,*
*And devils fear and fly.*

**Charles Wesley**

## MARK 5:14-20

# A short stay in Decapolis

Decapolis, the area to which Jesus and his disciples had come on the eastern side of the lake, was a semi-independent confederation of Greek towns, owing allegiance to Rome, but with little contact with Jewish culture and religion. Whatever Jesus' purpose in going across to this foreign territory, the stay now had to be cut short after what had happened with 'Legion'.

## Jesus is not welcome

There could be no doubt about the cure of the possessed man, and we might have thought that his compatriots would be grateful for his restoration and for the removal of a serious menace from the neighbourhood. But instead 'they were afraid'. The whole event has been too disturbing for them to think in such positive terms. This mysterious Jewish visitor is frightening, and will surely prove to be an uncomfortable person to have around. So, no doubt with due deference (you cannot afford to offend a man with such powers), they ask him to go back home. We may also reasonably assume that Jesus was *persona non grata* with the former owners of the drowned pigs! And Jesus does not argue, but gets straight back into the boat to return to the western shore.

## A potential disciple rejected

But what about 'Legion' himself? He owes everything to Jesus, and naturally enough he wants to stay with him. The use of the same phrase 'to be with him' as we saw in 3:14 suggests that he wants to join Jesus' permanent group of disciples, just like the twelve. And what better ambassador for Jesus could you imagine than a man who could give such a spectacular firsthand testimony to what Jesus' unique spiritual authority has done for him?

But Jesus has a more appropriate job for him. He is to stay in his own country and tell his own people about Jesus. Here in Decapolis, where he is known, he will have a more ready hearing than in the foreign territory of Jewish Galilee. It is in his own home and among his own people that he is to spread the news, and that is what he does, with great effect. Later in Mark's Gospel Jesus will come back to the same region (7:31—8:10), and the welcome he will then receive no doubt has a lot to do with the testimony of 'Legion' in the mean time.

## A breach of secrecy

There is a fascinating contrast between Jesus' desire to avoid publicity in Galilee (see 1:34, 44–45; 3:12 and the deliberately secret nature of his teaching portrayed in chapter 4) and the open encouragement of this man's testimony in Decapolis. There may have been all sorts of reasons for this which we do not now know, but perhaps it was due at least in part to the fact that this was away from Jesus' home area, and especially away from Jewish territory. The sheer practical difficulty posed by too great a popular following (1:45; 2:2) did not apply over here, since Jesus was not staying in the region. And in this Greek area there was no danger that his mission would be hijacked by a misdirected nationalistic enthusiasm for him as the Jewish messiah, a problem which was never far away in Galilee.

**PRAYER**

*Lord, help us to know what is the task you have for each of us, and not to assume that it will be the same as for others. And when we know it, may we, like 'Legion', undertake it gladly, and effectively.*

# 34 'Who touched me?'

Here again Mark tells a story within a story. It is as Jesus is on the way to respond to Jairus' request that he is delayed briefly by another remarkable incident. We shall return to Jairus in the next study.

## An embarrassing complaint

The 'haemorrhage' was presumably a menstrual disorder. Quite apart from the physical discomfort and weakness which resulted from it, for a Jewish woman it involved the further serious problem that a physical discharge rendered her ritually unclean, and therefore unable to take part in normal communal life (see Leviticus 15:25–31). After so many years it must have seemed incurable, and yet she is still determinedly seeking a cure. (It is perhaps not surprising that when Luke, the doctor, tells this story he does not echo Mark's wry comment on the shortcomings of the medical profession, verse 26!) Now there is a chance of a cure of a different sort, for she knows of Jesus' reputation as a miraculous healer. If only she can touch him.

But the touch of an 'unclean' woman is the last thing a religious teacher would want, as he too would then be made unclean for the rest of the day. So rather than confront him as other people did when they wanted to be healed, she comes up behind him, and touches the edge of his cloak, with the hope that even that minimal degree of contact will be enough. And it is!

## Unable to hide

But she has not reckoned with Jesus' supernatural knowledge. Among all the jostling crowd he has been aware of a single touch of a different kind, and is not prepared to let her get away with it in secret.

There is something oddly mechanical about the idea of feeling that 'power has gone out', as if 'power' was a physical substance, and a limited commodity to be used with care. Coupled with the woman's expectation that a mere touch on his cloak would be enough to secure healing, and her immediate physical sensation of being cured, it gives to this story a different 'feel' from Jesus' other healings. It sounds rather impersonal, even magical (though we shall see in 6:56 that this was not a unique case; cf. Acts 5:15; 19:12 for similarly 'impersonal' cures later). And perhaps it is true that her understanding of how Jesus could heal was of a more 'magical' type, and lacked theological sophistication. She would not have been alone in that.

Jesus has, perhaps involuntarily, responded to that limited understanding, but now he wants to put the relationship on a more personal basis. He wants to meet her openly, and she has no choice but to come forward. Yet she receives not the rebuke which she fears but a warm commendation and assurance that her cure is real and permanent. The key word, as so often in the accounts of Jesus' healings, is 'faith'. Rudimentary as it may have been, her faith has established a real relationship with her healer, and on that basis she is to be commended.

## FOR MEDITATION

*Put yourself in the woman's place. What would you have learned from this experience? And what might the disciples, as spectators, have learned about 'faith'?*

# 35 'Not dead, but sleeping'

After the unhappy confrontation the last time we heard of Jesus in the synagogue in Capernaum (3:1–6), it is a relief to find that at least one leading member of that institution still holds him in high regard, even if it is under the pressure of urgent personal need.

## Faith under pressure

Jairus, like others who meet Jesus in this Gospel, seems to have no doubt of the power of Jesus to heal. Even in the face of apparently imminent death, he takes it for granted that if Jesus will lay his hands on his daughter she will be restored and will not die. The only problem is to get him there in time. But the pressure of the crowd, and the delay in dealing with the woman with the haemorrhage, have held Jesus up for too long, and the report comes that the girl has died while he has been on the way. And, of course, death is death; there is no point in 'troubling the teacher any further'.

We are not told what Jairus himself felt when the news came. But Mark uses a conveniently ambiguous word for Jesus' response (v. 36): it could mean either that he 'overheard' the (private) message, or that he 'ignored' it. Certainly, he refuses to be put off, and summons Jairus to continuing faith rather than fear. We can only imagine the turmoil in Jairus' mind as he hurried on with Jesus to his house, on what must surely be a fool's errand.

## 'Get up, kid!'

Mark does not actually say that the girl was dead—only that everyone else thought she was dead. So it would be possible to take Jesus' words, 'Not dead, but sleeping', as simply a corrective diagnosis: they have mistaken a coma for death, and Jesus will now revive her from her 'sleep'. Matthew allows no such uncertainty: in his account Jairus does not appeal to Jesus until the girl is already dead (Matthew 9:18). And the way Mark tells the story, and the people's reaction, surely suggests that the death was real, and the revival

74

therefore a stupendous miracle, not a medical second opinion! In that case we must take Jesus' words not literally but as a way of saying that even death is not the end. 'They laughed at him' because they took his metaphorical words literally, and knew she was really dead.

The restoration of life is a majestic demonstration of Jesus' God-given authority, but the manner in which it is told is delightfully down-to-earth. The ejection of the sarcastic crowd, the small group at the bedside, and the simple act of taking the girl's hand are all as far as possible from the showmanship of a magician. The words 'Talitha cum' (in the vernacular Aramaic) are remarkably low-key: 'talitha' is literally a young sheep or goat but was used colloquially for a child, and 'cum' simply means 'Get up'. So 'Get up, kid!' is an idiomatic equivalent. And then there is the delightful final touch—she needs something to eat! But of course, what else would you do for someone just raised from the dead?!

Note again the avoidance of publicity, both in allowing only five people to witness the event, and in the strict instructions to keep it secret. Not that one could stop the neighbours talking when they met the dead girl in the street, but they were to be kept guessing as to just what happened and how it was done. Jesus is not in the business of becoming a travelling roadshow; he has more important things to do.

## PRAYER

*Lord, teach us what faith means when human possibilities are exhausted. May we not join the laughter of the crowd, but come into the little room in faith, even when we can have no idea what you are going to do.*

# 36

# A difficult visit to Nazareth

Nazareth was a small, rather insignificant village tucked away in the hills between the lake of Galilee and the Mediterranean, and away from the main centres of population. It was Jesus' home (1:9, 24), but for the whole of his public activity so far he has been based not in Nazareth but in the more populated area down by the lake some 20 miles away. He has recruited his disciples from the lakeside communities, and has made his base in Capernaum, where Simon and Andrew lived (and very likely in their home, 1:29).

## Familiarity breeds contempt

This is the first time Mark has told us of a visit to Nazareth since Jesus became a public figure. No doubt some news of his activities has found its way back to the village, but it has all been hearsay. Now for the first time they have a chance to hear and to assess the local boy who has been making a name for himself down by the lake.

An invitation to teach in the synagogue was not automatic, but for a distinguished visitor it would be an expected courtesy, and would naturally be extended to the local boy who has become so well known as a preacher in Capernaum, and has now returned home. And apparently they are not disappointed. Mark's verb 'astounded' indicates that they recognize in Jesus something out of the ordinary, and the references to his 'wisdom' (which they can hear for themselves) and his 'deeds of power' (about which they have heard reports) suggest that they are favourably impressed.

And yet they cannot accept him at face-value. How can a member of a local family, whom they have watched growing up and whose services they have employed as the village carpenter, turn out so differently from the rest of his family? We have already seen a similar response on the part of Jesus' family themselves (3:20–21, 31–35), and now the whole village shares in their scepticism. The problem, as with his family, is not outright hostility and rejection so much as

76

incomprehension. This sort of thing happens with other people from far away, not with a member of your own close-knit village community. Perhaps there is an element of jealousy, or at least the feeling that Jesus has become too big for his boots. And so 'they took offence at him'—the word means more literally 'they stumbled over him'.

## A disappointing home-coming

There is a note of pathos in Jesus' comment in verse 4. But it is a realistic observation. People do find it hard to recognize extraordinary qualities and powers in those they know best, and it is not every day that one of your neighbours turns out to be the herald of the kingdom of God, with power to raise the dead. Capernaum, which has known Jesus only as a remarkable preacher and healer, is likely to prove more fertile soil than Nazareth.

But even so it is startling to read that as a result Jesus *could not* work miracles in Nazareth (though Mark's give-away aside that he did in fact cure 'a few' sick people perhaps suggests that the difference was one of scale rather than of absolute impotence). But we have seen several times already in this Gospel the close link between faith and healing. Where there is no faith, where Jesus is not taken seriously, the necessary basis for healing is missing.

It is not often that we read of Jesus being 'amazed'. Other people were amazed by his power, but the only other time the verb is used of Jesus himself is in Matthew 8:10. There he was amazed by the faith of a stranger, here by the lack of faith among his own people.

It looks as though his visit to Nazareth was a short one. We do not know that he ever came back again.

### PRAYER

*Lord, save us from the prejudice which cannot rejoice in your work in those we know best. Give us the faith which can discern your presence even in the places we would least expect it.*

# 37

# The mission is extended

Jesus called the first four disciples in order to make them 'fish for people' (1:17), and he selected the twelve 'to be sent out to proclaim the message' (3:14). Now the time has come for them to take up that task.

## The nature of the task

Verses 12–13 give an overview of the disciples' mission. It includes the three main elements which we have seen to be characteristic of Jesus' own ministry so far, preaching, healing and exorcism. So this is not some new pattern of mission, but simply an extension, a multiplication, of what Jesus himself has already been doing. For some time the twelve have 'been with him' (3:14), and now they have his authority to do what he himself does. Not that they are now taking off on their own. It is as his emissaries, under his authority, that they are sent, and in verse 30 they will report back to him as their 'director'.

It is nonetheless remarkable that what we have so far come to think of as the unique authority of Jesus as the Son of God is in fact able to be delegated in this way to his very fallible associates. But of course this is what has been happening ever since. Once Jesus himself was removed from the earthly scene such a 'delegation of authority' would become essential, but already while he is still around he is willing to trust these 'learners' with an amazing level of responsibility.

As in Jesus' own ministry the authority over unclean spirits features prominently in their 'job description'—more prominently indeed than preaching! And as we have seen already, exorcism is carefully distinguished in verse 13 from the healing of physical illness. What is unusual here is the mention of anointing with oil as apparently a normal method of physical healing. There is no record that Jesus ever anointed the sick. Indeed the only other reference to the practice in the New Testament is in James 5:14 (where again it seems to be accepted as normal). Anointing is in other contexts a symbol of God's blessing, and perhaps it is used by the disciples as a way of assuring their 'patients' of the love and power of the God on whom they depend for healing. When Jesus himself was present, there was no need for such assurance.

## Travelling light

The detailed instructions in verses 8–11 emphasize the need to travel light. They are not to take provisions or spare equipment, but to depend on the hospitality offered by well-wishers wherever they go (as indeed Jesus and the whole disciple group are already in the habit of doing). In the Middle East this is not such an impractical programme as it might seem in our society, since hospitality to strangers is a sacred duty. There is the possibility that in some places they may not be welcome (v. 11), but such rejection is clearly exceptional, and is to be marked by a vivid gesture of disassociation. If it happens, it will be on account of the startling message they are sent to proclaim ('they refuse to hear you'), and anyone who will not listen to the call to repent in view of the coming of the kingdom of God needs to be shown in no uncertain terms the gravity of their decision.

In one way the situation of the twelve at this time was unique. But there are elements in their commission which apply to all disciples of Jesus through the ages: the privilege of sharing the master's own mission, the authority he gives, the sense of urgency and of the importance of the message of the kingdom of God. In many different settings these are the experience of Christians all over the world today, as they have always been.

### PRAYER

*We are amazed, Lord, at the privilege of sharing your mission. Thank you that with the commission comes the authority to fulfil it. Help us in our day to find the right way to undertake it, and to proclaim your message to those around us where we are.*

# Jesus and
# John the Baptist

## A change of scene

The disciples, sent out on their mission in verses 7–13, will return and report back in verse 30. The intervening space is filled with an unexpected return to the person with whom Mark's story began. We left John the Baptist after his arrest in 1:14, and since that time we have heard nothing of him (except a brief reference to his followers in 2:18); if we have thought about him at all, we have been left to assume that he is languishing in prison, though we have so far been given no clue as to why he has run into trouble. His time of public acclaim is over, and Jesus has become the centre of attention.

So a return to John at this stage is surprising, the more so because in verses 17–29 the focus will be entirely on John, and Jesus will be temporarily out of the picture altogether. Those verses will, no doubt, satisfy our curiosity as to what has happened to John and why, but they seem an unnecessary digression in the story of Jesus.

But the three verses which introduce the 'digression' give us a clue as to why it is here. In verses 14–16 we discover that in popular opinion Jesus was widely seen as a second John the Baptist (the same idea will emerge in 8:28). The close link between their two missions may not be much emphasized in the story proper, for the very good reason that John was already in prison when Jesus began to appear in public. But Mark does not want us to forget the context in which Jesus began his preaching, and in 11:27–33 the parallel between the two men will be an important testimony to the divine authority with which Jesus himself is endowed. And of course the violent end which John has met is an ominous forewarning of what will happen to his successor (as Jesus will himself declare in 9:11–13). So John is not to be forgotten (even though Mark's gift for telling a good story does perhaps lead him to give the story of John's death a prominence which is a bit out of proportion!).

# Herod Antipas

The 'Herod' of this story is not Herod the Great (who died soon after Jesus was born), but his son Antipas who ruled Galilee (as a protégé of the Romans) during the time of Jesus' ministry. It is his bizarre idea that Jesus is John the Baptist returned to life which gives Mark the excuse to tell us the story of John's end.

Herod was not the only one to link the popular preacher and healer Jesus with the equally popular preacher John. The general public, trying to make sense of the Jesus phenomenon, naturally turned to John as a model (and may well have known that John had talked of a 'more powerful' successor to follow him). And John, as we have seen, was above all a prophet, a man who fearlessly proclaimed God's message and was recognized as having a special authority and charisma. We have seen too that John's mission was to some degree modelled on that of Elijah—and Elijah was expected to return to usher in the great Day of the Lord. So all this adds up to a potent mixture of ideas all focused now on Jesus, the one through whom God's voice is now being heard.

But for Herod all this talk of prophecy and of John coming back from the dead has a much more sinister ring, because it is he who has been responsible for the execution of the earlier 'prophet', and now he fears that his victim is coming back to haunt him. For a petty ruler whose insecurity has already led him to eliminate one popular leader, this is a frightening prospect. It may well be that Herod would in due course have a hand in the plot to get rid of Jesus, (and indeed Mark includes a few references to him and his supporters as opponents of Jesus: 3:6; 8:15; 12:13), but after this brief glimpse of Herod's fear he will not bring him into his narrative again.

## FOR MEDITATION

*Herod and the general public illustrate some of the ways popular superstition tried to make sense of Jesus. In what ways do people today try to pigeonhole Jesus, and how can their ideas best be developed or corrected?*

# 39

# The dance of death

In the previous study we thought about why this story is here, and why Mark may have felt it appropriate to insert it into the story of Jesus. But now we shall look at the story of the death of John in its own right. It is, of course, a 'flashback'; we do not know how soon after his arrest John was executed, but it was while Jesus was still publicly preaching in Galilee.

## Why John was in prison

The Jewish historian Josephus tells us that Herod executed John because he knew of his popularity, and feared that he might become the leader of a rebellion against him. (He also says that such was John's popularity that a subsequent military defeat of Herod's army was explained by popular opinion as divine retribution for his having executed John.) But Mark gives us another and more personal reason, in Herod's annoyance (and bad conscience?) over John's criticism of his marriage to Herodias, and the implacable hostility of Herodias herself. Herod had divorced his wife in order to marry Herodias, and Herodias had left her husband, who was Herod's half-brother. In Jewish law a woman had no right to divorce her husband, and when you add the close family relations involved in this double 'divorce' and remarriage it is no wonder that people were scandalized. John's robust denunciation was, no doubt, in tune with popular opinion, and that made it doubly wounding, and dangerous, for Herod and Herodias.

And yet Herod himself comes across in this story as irresolute, and will not take action until he is forced into a corner. Verse 20 suggests at least an uneasy conscience, and even a perverse pleasure in listening to his tormentor. Moreover, knowing that other people thought John to be 'righteous and holy' (and a prophet of God too!), he must at least have been aware of the political danger in eliminating him; perhaps he himself really shared that opinion of John. Without Herodias to act as his Lady Macbeth he might have hesitated for a long time.

# The death of John

Apart from John's bold and uncompromising stand for principle, there is nothing admirable in this story. It is a notorious and sordid example of intrigue and licentiousness at the court of a minor oriental potentate. Mark tells the story vividly and with gusto, but we are mercifully spared the more lurid details with which tradition has invested the story of the princess's dance.

But John himself appears only as a passive victim, summarily executed off the stage in order to appease the anger of the wicked 'queen'. It is a sadly inglorious end to the life of a man who had had such a powerful impact for good on the society of his time, and from whose ministry the mission of Jesus was born.

## FOR MEDITATION

*We are left to ponder on the nature of a world where evil can so openly triumph, and where virtue and courage, and even the call of God to a prophetic ministry, are no protection against petty self-interest in high places. But it is a salutary reminder at this stage in the story of the Son of God who will all too soon be setting out determinedly on the road which leads inevitably to Golgotha.*

# 40 An abortive 'retreat'

This is the only time in Mark's Gospel that the Twelve are called 'apostles'. The word means 'those sent out', and it describes well the experience they have just shared as Jesus' emissaries. But having been 'sent out', they now return and report back to the one who sent them, and now that they are back with him they will again be described by their more common name, 'disciples', that is 'learners'. It is the balance between learning and being sent out which will be the secret of their effectiveness as Jesus' task force for mission.

## The need for retreat

And now it is time for 'learning' again. They have been through a demanding and exhausting time of mission, and it is time to recharge. Jesus' words in verse 31 could hardly be more emphatic: 'Come away', 'a deserted place', 'all by yourselves', 'rest'. It has been the experience of Christian people down the ages that such a time of withdrawal from the pressures of everyday activity is needed from time to time, even if the 'deserted places' may not always be found by geographical isolation. And the more the pressure of responsibility the greater the need for retreat. Some Christians, governed by the 'Protestant work ethic', have thought of 'rest' as at best a concession to human weakness, to be enjoyed, if at all, only with an underlying sense of guilt. Jesus and his disciples had no such inhibitions!

## The retreat is frustrated

Mark has told us several times of the popularity of Jesus among ordinary people, but here is the most remarkable example of it. We might have thought, as no doubt the disciples did, that an escape by boat should secure the privacy they wanted, but so eager were the people to catch up with Jesus again that they set off along the shore, tracking the progress of the boat, and were there waiting for them when they disembarked.

Jesus would have had every excuse for complaining at the invasion of privacy and refusing to be available, but instead we read of his 'compassion', which leads him to drop the plans for a retreat and launch again into an extended period of teaching. We can only guess what the disciples thought of this!

## Why this persistence?

In verse 44 we read that the five thousand who followed Jesus around the lake-shore were 'men' (the word is specifically masculine: Matthew adds 'without women and children'). What motivated so large a group of men to make this impromptu journey to meet Jesus in the wilderness, when they (and their families) could apparently hear him preaching in Capernaum any time? John tells us that after the feeding miracle they tried to 'take Jesus by force to make him king' (John 6:15). Mark is not so explicit, but there are a few hints: 'sheep without a shepherd' (v. 34) is used in 1 Kings 22:17 for an army without a commander, and the division of the crowd into numbered ranks (v. 40) has a military flavour.

It is quite likely, then, that the reason this large male contingent chased him into the wilderness (the traditional place for a nationalistic uprising) was that they had come to the conclusion that he was the charismatic figure they needed to lead them against the Roman occupation, and that it was more than teaching they were looking for. The fact that Jesus will pack the disciples off so hastily in the boat in verse 45 may suggest that they too were in danger of being caught up in the nationalistic fervour. The danger of being hijacked into leading a political insurrection is never far away from Jesus in Mark's Gospel, and here it may well be that the issue was coming to a head.

### FOR MEDITATION
*What practical guidance may we draw for our own lives from*
*(a) Jesus' intention to take his disciples into a retreat and*
*(b) his response when the plan was foiled?*

# 41 Food in the wilderness

## Bread from heaven

When Israel were hungry in the wilderness under the leadership of
Moses, they were given 'bread from heaven' to eat, in the form of
manna (Exodus 16). The prophet Elisha once fed a hundred people
with a mere twenty loaves (a 'loaf' in these stories is more like what
we would call a 'roll', enough for one person at most), and there was
still some left over (2 Kings 4:42–44). Now Jesus will perform a miracle on a far greater scale than Elisha's, and the comparison with
Moses, the great leader who had made Israel into a nation, must
inevitably be made. If it was a charismatic leader they were looking
for, surely here was another Moses.

If that was how the five thousand men saw it, however, it does not
seem to have been Jesus' intention, nor is it the message Mark wants
his readers to take away from this amazing story. Jesus' motive is
'compassion' for a hungry crowd, not a desire to display divine
power, or establish a claim to leadership.

## Much from little

From the disciples' point of view, this was a lesson in faith (and one
which Jesus will later expect them to have learned: 8:17–21). Jesus'
challenge to them to provide enough food is ludicrous—the food
simply is not available even if they could afford to buy it. The
amount they can actually lay their hands on is not enough to
feed even the disciple group themselves, let alone their vast crowd
of uninvited guests. We can guess their bewilderment and embarrassment when they have to get the crowd sitting down ready for a
picnic—of what?

But they have to go through with it, and Jesus deliberately
involves them all the way through, in preparing the crowd, in serving the food, and in gathering up the leftovers (which are far more
than there was to start with!). The carefully preserved numbers (five
rolls, two fish, twelve baskets, five thousand men) reflect their amaze-

ment as they went round with their twelve baskets collecting up the impossible remains. They would never forget any detail of this experience.

## A foretaste of the future

Mark's readers can see in this story something else which the disciples could not see at the time. The verbs in verse 41 ('Take', 'bless', 'break', 'give') are the same verbs which will be used at each account of the Last Supper, where Jesus will institute a memorial meal for Christians to observe in memory of him. Christianity has a shared meal at the centre of its worship, and Christians accustomed to this observance cannot fail to see in this impromptu meal shared beside the lake a foretaste of the eucharistic feast of the kingdom of God. And, having recognized this symbolic dimension, we note with approval that all who ate this meal, small as its provisions had been, were fully satisfied. So it is with the eucharistic bread from heaven.

### FOR MEDITATION

*Jesus said to them, '... it was not Moses who gave you the bread from heaven, but it is my Father who gives you the true bread from heaven. For the bread of God is that which comes down from heaven and gives life to the world.' They said to him, 'Sir, give us this bread always.' Jesus said to them, 'I am the bread of life. Whoever comes to me will never be hungry.'*
**John 6:32–35**

# Panic on the lake

## What Jesus did next

If our speculations about the insurrectionary atmosphere in the wilderness were right, the disciples, fresh from the amazing experience of the loaves and fish, may well have shared the crowd's hopes and enthusiasm, and wanted Jesus to declare himself as the new Moses. But Jesus has no such intention, and instead packs the disciples off as quickly as possible in the boat, away from the excited crowd. As for the crowd themselves, Jesus simply 'dismissed' them. We cannot know how much is hidden behind that little word, but it may well have been one of the supreme tests of Jesus' authority to pacify such a large and eager crowd, and to be able to get away from them by himself.

But for Jesus the priority is prayer. As in 1:35, he needs to get away alone with his Father, and to clarify his vision of the task he has come to fulfil. If *Jesus* needed this, even at a time of such hectic activity, what does that imply for the rest of us?

## Meanwhile, out on the lake

It cannot have been much more than three or four miles back by boat to the Capernaum area, but the conditions are so bad that even experienced fishermen are still far out on the lake in the early hours of the morning. Exhausted and frightened, they are in no state to cope with the vision of a human figure walking over the waves in the dim pre-dawn light, and they assume it is a ghost. Once again, Jesus is doing what is impossible, and it is hardly surprising that they cannot recognize him, or realize the miracle that is taking place, until he speaks to them.

They have been in a storm on the lake before (4:35–41), but that time they had Jesus with them. Now when he joins them in the boat, again the danger is over, and the storm subsides. But the quelling of the storm is mentioned this time almost as an afterthought, overshadowed by the amazing feat of walking on a stormy lake. Of course there have been attempts to explain away the miracle, by picturing Jesus wading in the surf by the shore, or walking on a hidden sandbank. But experienced fishermen would know their lake better than that, and Mark clearly has no doubt that the boat is far from the shore. Following on the equally impossible event of the multiplying of the bread and fish, this is undoubtedly presented to us as a miracle. Certainly that was how the disciples understood it.

## Hard hearts?

And yet Mark adds the rather harsh comment that they still did not understand, because their hearts were hardened. We might well wonder whether any of us would have scored any more highly in such circumstances. It is not easy to take miracles for granted, especially where, as in this case, nothing of the sort has happened before. Mark apparently expects them to have learned something from 'the loaves' which would have prepared them also for this quite different encounter with supernatural power. He will return to the theme more fully in 8:14–21, and in the following chapters we shall see again and again how difficult the disciples found it to adapt to the new realities and values of the kingdom of God. But at this point we may have a good deal of sympathy with them: there is a limit to how much impossibility one can absorb in a short time!

**PRAYER**

*Lord, make us ready to be surprised by you, and help us not to try to limit you to what we can grasp.*

# 43

# More healings

Once again Mark allows us a brief respite from the breathless series of amazing events. This more general summary of what Jesus was doing in Galilee at this period, like that in 3:7-12, shows us that the relatively few specific miracles which he has included in his story are part of a much more wide-ranging ministry. But general as this summary may be, it still breathes an air of restless activity and excitement. Nothing is ever ordinary when Jesus is around.

## Healing at Gennesaret

Capernaum was Jesus' base, and it was probably from there that he and his disciples had set out on their abortive retreat. They return now to Gennesaret, a few miles further down the west shore of the lake. But it is close enough to Capernaum for Jesus to be well known, and immediately the people of this area seize their opportunity to benefit in their turn from the presence of the famous healer.

In this summary Mark makes no mention of either teaching or exorcism, the other main components of Jesus' ministry as he has presented it so far. From the point of view of ordinary people, no doubt, it was the possibility of healing which was the most immediate hope when someone like Jesus came along. And the hope is amply fulfilled: 'all who touched were healed'.

## Touching the fringe of his cloak

Perhaps the news of how the woman with the haemorrhage was healed (5:24-34) has got around, and people have concluded that touching Jesus' cloak is the proper way to seek for healing! They clearly believe that his healing power is such that the patient does not need a lengthy personal encounter with Jesus. We might look rather askance at such a 'magical' approach to healing, but presumably we are to understand that those who touched and were healed were motivated by the same sort of faith as Jesus commended in the woman who had pioneered this sort of approach. It is faith, not the technique which is followed, which is the basis of healing. The contrast with Nazareth (v. 5) is striking. Here people may have had little idea of who Jesus really was, but they came to him with real faith, not with the scepticism which we have seen in his fellow-villagers at Nazareth.

## FOR MEDITATION

*This little passage offers us the opportunity to pause and reflect on what we have learned so far about Jesus' ministry in Galilee.*

*Try to put yourself into the place of (a) an ordinary villager in Capernaum or Gennesaret and (b) one of Jesus' disciples, and ask yourself what you would have made of Jesus by this point. What would be the things that most excited and most puzzled you? How much would you have been able to see for yourself of the coming of the kingdom of God, and of Jesus as the Son of God?*

# 44 What is purity?

The last time we met scribes who had come from Jerusalem to Galilee to confront Jesus (3:22) their arrival spelt trouble. Here again they are a hostile group, a foretaste of the sort of reception Jesus is going to meet when he eventually goes to Jerusalem himself. The issue of purity which they raise is one which will fundamentally divide Jesus from the religious establishment, and it is important enough for Mark to devote a long section directly to the discussion (vv. 1–23), while the stories that follow will illustrate the way Jesus' mission inevitably takes him outside the 'pure' boundaries of Israel, into company which would scandalize the scribes.

## The tradition of the elders

Ritual purity, the ways in which it may be lost, and the procedure necessary to restore it, are major themes in the Old Testament law. Those Jews who wished to remain ceremonially 'clean' (and therefore able to take part in worship and in social activities) had to be careful about whom they encountered, what they ate and touched, and about their own bodily condition.

In the Old Testament the formal washing of hands before eating was prescribed only for priests, but by the time of Jesus the keener type of Jews (particularly the Pharisees) had adopted this as a requirement for themselves and for anyone else they could influence to follow them. Mark's broad-brush comment on Jewish practice in verses 3–4 exaggerates a little, but this is the way things were moving. So surely Jesus, as a professed religious leader, could be expected to be equally strict with his own followers. If he ignored this (recently developed!) 'tradition of the elders' he could not be taken seriously as a religious teacher.

## A matter of priorities

We shall hear what Jesus has to say directly about the issue of purity when we come to verse 15. But first he has some more general comments to make on the status of the 'tradition of the elders'. The scribes' question (v. 5) contained a veiled threat, but Jesus launches into a direct and stinging attack on their whole approach to religious observance. They are 'hypocrites', a word which sometimes in the Gospels means what we mean by it—insincere people who put on an act—but also goes further to include those who have got things disastrously out of proportion, who think they are doing the will of God when in fact they are doing just the opposite.

Their 'hypocrisy' is defined in Isaiah's scathing words about his own contemporaries, whose supposed worship was all on the surface, and who paid more attention to their own human religious traditions than they did to knowing and loving God himself. The same is true, Jesus implies, of these scribes, who are more concerned to uphold their 'tradition of the elders' than to find out what God really wants from them. Indeed, he goes further: they actually abandon God's declared will, and put their own human traditions in its place. Just how they do this will be explored in the next study.

## PRAYER

*Save us, O God, from putting our own or other people's ideas of what is right before what you have revealed to us as your will, and give us the wisdom to discern the difference.*

MARK 7:9-13

# 45 Putting the cart before the horse

## 'Making void the word of God'

The unexpected accusation which Jesus has launched against the
scribes in verse 8 is repeated in different words twice more, in verses
9 and 13. The 'tradition' of which they are so proud, and which
they see as the key to living as God requires, in fact has quite the
opposite effect, and *prevents* people from living according to God's
law. The terms used, 'commandment of God', 'word of God', underline the seriousness of the charge. God has plainly declared his will,
and they are undermining it by setting up their own rules and regulations. 'Tradition', which can and should be a helpful guide to how
we may apply God's laws to the realities of everyday life, has a dangerous tendency to develop a life of its own, and when it does it
becomes an enemy rather than a friend. That is what has happened
to the scribes.

## An offering to God?

The particular example Jesus chooses to establish his charge involves
a complex area of scribal law. The formula 'Corban' (dedicated) was
used to set something aside from common use. It became, in theory,
the property of God to whom it was dedicated, and so was not available to anyone else. But it is easy to see how this formula could be
abused by someone whose motive was not really to give anything to
God but to keep it out of the reach of other people. And it seems that
this device was being applied, with the consent of the scribes, to family disputes about property.

Respect for parents, and therefore the obligation to provide for
them when they were no longer able to look after themselves, was a
basic principle of Israelite society, enshrined in the Fifth
Commandment. An aging parent should be able to look forward
with confidence to the care and material support of sons and

94

daughters. But a selfish son could apparently declare his property 'Corban', and so remove it from his parents' reach. It seems likely that some device had been contrived to enable him nonetheless to retain the use of it himself even after it had been declared the property of God. The whole system was a fiddle, cynically manipulating the religious ideal of giving to God in the interests of sheer selfishness. And the scribes, apparently, not only connived at it, but even directly forbade the son to give any help to his parents once the formula had been invoked (v. 12). There is a good deal of discussion in the Mishnah about how, if at all, such a vow could be repealed, and in at least some cases the rabbis declared it impossible, even where the son who made the vow had now changed his mind and wanted to help his parents. So much for the Fifth Commandment!

All this has nothing to do with purity: we shall come back to that issue in the next study. But it shows how easily the scribes' meticulous concern for rules and regulations could end up by not only ignoring but even undermining the 'weightier matters' (Matthew 23:23). Knowingly or not, the same concern for ritual detail which had led them to criticize the eating habits of Jesus' disciples had made them 'hypocrites' with regard to family responsibilities.

## FOR MEDITATION

*In what ways are we also in danger of putting the cart before the horse, by focusing on minor externals and forgetting the things that really matter, and by putting our traditions before the word of God?*

# Clean hands and a pure heart

We now return to the issue which sparked off this sharp dialogue, that of purity. Jesus declares his position by means of a 'parable' (which means here an epigram or a puzzling saying needing interpretation—see our study of chapter 4), which, following the pattern established in chapter 4, he then goes on to explain to his disciples.

## Not what goes in but what comes out

The purity laws of the Old Testament were all based on the principle that uncleanness is contracted by touching and eating unclean things. In other words, the impurity is there 'outside' the person and 'comes in', rendering the person unclean. It is this basic principle which Jesus here questions and indeed turns completely on its head. Impurity is already there 'inside', and 'comes out' in what a person says and does.

It is difficult for us to appreciate what a radical reorientation this pronouncement involves for those brought up in a culture which has never questioned the principle of 'external defilement'. The laws regulating what food is clean or unclean were one of the main distinguishing marks of the Jews, and severely limited the social contact they might have with those outside Israel. To observe them carefully was, for many Jews, a matter of patriotic pride as well as religious obligation.

## How far did Jesus mean to go?

Of course it was not the Old Testament food laws that the scribes had questioned Jesus about, but rather the relatively insignificant issue of washing hands before meals (which was not in itself an Old Testament regulation for anyone except priests). But Jesus has deliberately responded in a much more general vein, repudiating not merely the practice of ritual washing, but the whole concept of external defilement on which it and the Old Testament food laws were based. His rather crude depiction of what happens to the food we eat in the first part of verse 19 indicates that food as such cannot be regarded as the source of defilement: it is merely a temporary visitor to the body.

Mark adds at the end of verse 19 his own editorial comment, 'Thus he declared all foods clean.' For Mark, then the implications of Jesus' 'parable' were clear: the Old Testament food laws no longer apply. The result of this is, of course, to remove at a stroke one of the major obstacles to fellowship between Jew and Gentile, and one which was to be the focus of a lot of controversy in the early years of the church as we see in the book of Acts, until the Christians eventually came to accept that Jew and Gentile must be accepted on an equal footing in the kingdom of God.

Jesus did not actually say that in so many words, and perhaps that is why some of his followers were so slow to get the point (like Peter in Acts 10:9–16). But it is hard to see what else he could have intended by so general a declaration as verse 15.

## Inner purity

Verses 21–23 are a sad commentary on what human nature is capable of. Not that these are the *only* products of 'the heart', but they are only too familiar. In the light of such 'uncleanness', ritual purity becomes irrelevant. To meditate on these vices (and their corresponding virtues) is to take us to the heart of what true religion is really about.

**PRAYER**

*Create in me a clean heart, O God,
and put a new and right spirit within me.*
**Psalm 51:10**

# 47 Crumbs for the Gentiles

The question of purity, discussed in the first part of this chapter, would have important repercussions for the eventual expansion of the church to contain Gentiles alongside the original Jewish believers. This strange little story illustrates the point, as the Jewish teacher is confronted by a cry for help from an 'unclean' Gentile woman.

## An unlikely request

Jesus' attempts to escape from public attention are constantly doomed to failure. Even in Phoenician territory to the north of Galilee, the home of Israel's traditional enemies, he is sought out by someone in need. It is hard to imagine a more inappropriate request, from a traditional Jewish point of view. As a religious teacher Jesus should not have any dealings with a woman, or with a Gentile, and the fact that her daughter is possessed by an 'unclean spirit' compounds the problem. Other rabbis would have turned from her in horror.

## An unsympathetic response?

Jesus does at least listen to her request. But his first words are far from encouraging, and indeed they sound quite brutal. The woman and her daughter are, apparently, classed as 'dogs'. It is true that the Greek word means a little dog, but that does not help much, as a dog of any size was for the Jews an unclean animal, and the term 'dogs' was a traditional and deliberately offensive Jewish way of describing Gentiles.

It is remarkable that the woman does not give up there and then. The fact that she persists, and in the end is rewarded for her perseverance, may suggest that there was something about the way Jesus said these rough words which indicated that he was hoping for a reply. This is the sort of response which long experience of Jewish-Gentile hostility must have led her to expect from a Jewish teacher, but was he perhaps testing her with this stock answer to see whether she could rise above it? And that is exactly what she does.

## A clever reply

Rather than protest against Jesus' use of such an unwelcome term she turns it against him. If we Gentiles are dogs, then even dogs have their rights. They may be second-class citizens, but they too are fed. The children do not eat all the food; there is some left for the dogs.

It is a clever development of Jesus' imagery, but it is more than that. Jesus is the Messiah of Israel, and his mission to Israel is the primary focus of his ministry. The children do indeed have the first priority. But she is perceptive enough to realize that Jesus' mission is broader than that. Perhaps she has seized especially on his word 'first'. If the feeding of the children comes first, what then? Then it will be time for the dogs! Here, in a nutshell, is the pattern of the Christian mission in New Testament times, 'to the Jew first and also to the Greek [i.e. Gentile]' (Romans 1:16).

## A happy ending

'For saying that', and thus revealing her grasp of his special situation as Israel's Messiah without abandoning her hope that she as a Gentile also has a claim on his attention, her request is granted. And who is to say that that is not what Jesus intended all along, despite the apparent coldness of his first reply? She has passed the test with flying colours, and is rewarded by one of the most remarkable miracles in Mark's story, an exorcism not by face-to-face confrontation but by 'remote control'.

**PRAYER**

*Lord, give us the faith to discern your purpose for us, and so to pray on in spite of apparent refusal.*

# 48 Another Gentile healed

The previous story focused on the question of Jesus' mission to Gentiles as well as Jews. Now we see him continuing in Gentile territory: Sidon, like Tyre, was Phoenician, and Decapolis was the Greek-dominated area to the east of the lake of Galilee (see on 5:14–20). So while the racial origin of the deaf man is not made an issue in this story, we are surely right to assume that again it is a Gentile who benefits from the healing power of the Messiah of Israel. (Matthew at this point, 15:31, tells how the crowds 'praised the God of Israel', which sounds like a Gentile reaction.)

## 'He makes the deaf to hear'

Deafness and dumbness (or a serious speech impediment: note the expression 'his tongue was released' in verse 35) are complaints which have not yet been mentioned specifically, though they may well have been included in the general summaries of Jesus' healing ministry. To heal such a person would have special significance in the light of Isaiah 35:5–6 where the blessings of the age to come include: 'Then shall the ears of the deaf be unstopped... and the tongue of the speechless sing for joy'. These things are to happen when *God* comes to save his people—and here they are happening at the hands of Jesus!

Mark tells the story in unusual detail (though he will give quite a similar account of the healing of a blind man in 8:22–26). Here we read not merely of Jesus touching or speaking to the patient, but more specifically of his touching the organs affected, and using saliva as part of the cure (as also in 8:23). This more elaborate method in place of a simple word of healing would of course be particularly appropriate for a deaf man. The use of saliva as a healing agent, which seems strange to us, was quite common in the ancient world, sometimes in a more magical healing ritual, but sometimes in quite ordinary medical practice.

But there is also an authoritative word of healing, 'Be opened'. The fact that Mark records it in the original Aramaic as well as in

Greek (as he did in 5:41) suggests that people remembered this ring-ing command—and no doubt so did the man himself, as the first word he had ever heard.

## The command to silence—again

The fact that the local people have brought the man to Jesus expect-ing him to cure him indicates that his reputation has spread into this Gentile area. It may well have been quite close to where 'Legion' had been delivered from his demon-possession, and after that incident Jesus had told him to go back and tell people about what had hap-pened (5:19–20). It looks as if he has done so very effectively, and when Jesus reappears in their region they are ready for him. So it is surprising that this time Jesus again tries to avoid publicity, as we have seen him doing several times in Jewish areas. He carries out the cure in private, and afterwards asks the people not to talk about it—and again they take no notice!

Jesus' previous commands to silence seem to have been in order to avoid too much popular enthusiasm among his own people, who might have their own ideas as to what sort of Messiah they wanted him to be. But perhaps by this time even among Gentiles his repu-tation as a healer is getting out of hand. He has other priorities in his mission, and from this point on we shall hear much less of his heal-ing and much more of his teaching, particularly his private teaching of the disciples. In the long term this, rather than an extended heal-ing campaign, will be what counts for the future.

### PRAYER

*Lord, you have done everything well. You even make the deaf to hear and the mute to speak. Cause us too to hear your voice and to speak of you, so that others may find your saving power.*

# 49
# Food for the
# Gentiles too

## Why another impromptu feast?

Only a page or two ago Mark has told a story of the miraculous feeding of a large crowd of men. Now he tells another story, similar in general outline, but different in detail, particularly in the numbers (4,000 people instead of 5,000 men; seven loaves and a few small fish instead of five and two; seven baskets instead of twelve). Why the repetition? Is Mark so short of material that he has to tell the same story twice?

But of course it is not the same story, and in 8:19-21 Jesus will make the point that there were two such incidents, not just one. So there must be some importance in the fact that Jesus did it twice.

## 'The dogs eat the children's crumbs'

Perhaps we should find the clue in the fact that since 7:24 Jesus has been moving in Gentile territory. Here he is, apparently, still in the region of Decapolis, from which he and the disciples will return to the Jewish shore of the lake in verse 10. In that case, whereas the crowd of five thousand whom he fed in 6:35-44 were Jews, these four thousand are predominantly Gentiles.

Is there a pointer to this deliberate extension of Jesus' ministry outside Israel in the strange dialogue between Jesus and the Gentile woman in 7:27-28? There is bread for the children, but there is also bread for the dogs. The bread which Jesus provided for the large Jewish crowd is now matched by bread for the Gentiles. The scale of the miracle is a little reduced (fewer people fed from a slightly more ample supply, and not so much left over), but we are still in the realm of the impossible. The 'children's crumbs' turn out to be an ample feast after all.

# A pointer to the future

This miracle brings us to the end of the short section of Mark's Gospel in which he tells of Jesus' ministry among non-Jewish people (7:24—8:9). After this point Jesus will be among Jewish people; when he takes the disciples into Gentile territory again in 8:27 it will not be to conduct a mission among the local people, but to find a quiet place where he can concentrate on teaching his own disciples. When he returns to Jewish territory it will be as the Jewish Messiah that he will eventually come to the Jewish capital and be rejected by the leadership of the Jewish people.

But those who have seen the significance of this little section will know that that is not the end of the story. What Jesus has symbolically enacted by feeding a Gentile crowd as well as a Jewish one will soon become a more lasting reality, as his disciples will, reluctantly and uncertainly at first, but with increasing determination, take the gospel of salvation to all nations. When they look back on this incident, so little understood at the time, they will see in it a mandate for their universal mission. The Messiah of Israel is the saviour of the world.

## PRAYER

*Lord Jesus, help us to share the breadth of your vision, and to know that your blessings are for all people, and not only for our own group.*

# 50 Asking for a sign

When Jesus left Galilee in 7:24 he had been engaged in sharp debate with the Pharisees and scribes, and the dialogue had ended with Jesus making a radical pronouncement about purity which must have left his opponents seething, since he was apparently taking it upon himself to undermine a basic principle of the Old Testament law, and one on which much of their professional expertise depended. So now when he comes back to the Jewish side of the lake they are ready for him.

## A sign from heaven

Their request for a sign is on the face of it quite legitimate. Often in the Old Testament signs (usually some form of miraculous occurrence) were given in order to authenticate one who claimed to have a mission from God. Moses was given 'signs' to perform in order to convince the sceptics (Exodus 4:1–9), and Isaiah invited Ahaz to ask for one (Isaiah 7:10–11). Given the contentious nature of what Jesus has been saying, it might therefore seem wise on the part of the Pharisees to ask for his credentials in the same way. But Mark indicates that their motivation is not a dispassionate search for truth. They have come 'to argue with him', 'to test him'.

The sign they are looking for is one 'from heaven'. It must make it quite clear that he has God's approval and authority. Mark's readers know, of course, that God has already declared that Jesus is his Son, in whom he is well pleased (1:11). The people of these villages, however, have not heard that direct declaration. Even so, might we not expect that they would be convinced by the extraordinary sequence of miraculous happenings which have surrounded Jesus' ministry? Some of those miracles have been very public, and have made him the talk of the town. What more can they ask?

# No sign for this generation

Perhaps this group of Pharisees has not been personally present at any of these alleged miracles, and they are not prepared to trust to hearsay. Or they may be thinking that even miraculous events may have more than one explanation, just as the scribes in 3:22 attributed Jesus' exorcisms to the power of Satan, not to God. But Jesus' response indicates that their request is not sincere, and that no sign would be of any value in the face of determined scepticism. There is to be no sign for this generation.

And with that 'he left them'. Galilee and its religious leaders have seen the last of Jesus. Thus Act 1 of Mark's drama draws to its close. Now Jesus is going away on a journey which will ultimately take him to the even more hostile territory of Judea, and to his death in Jerusalem. Galilee has had its opportunity, and Jesus will not go on appealing for ever to those who do not want to be convinced. 'This generation' has made its choice.

## FOR MEDITATION

*How much 'proof', and of what sort, is it legitimate for us to expect from God? What is the balance between proof and faith? In what circumstances might it be appropriate for us to decide that no further evidence should be offered to those who are not willing to be convinced?*

## MARK 8:14-21
# Difficult questions on the lake

Act 1 finishes with an enigmatic little scene on the lake as Jesus and his disciples go away from Galilee. Its connecting theme is bread, but it takes some lateral thinking to follow how the dialogue develops. Bread has, of course, been a prominent motif in recent chapters, the literal bread of the two feeding miracles and the metaphorical bread which is for the children not for the dogs. Mark has already warned us that the disciples have failed to understand 'about the loaves' (6:52), and now that lack of understanding will be more fully exposed.

## Bread and yeast

The setting is down to earth enough. The disciples realize that they have set off on their journey with no more than a single small bread roll in the boat. When they hear Jesus talking about yeast they immediately assume that he is commenting on their failure to make proper provision. They are so preoccupied with their problem that they fail to see that Jesus is not talking about literal bread at all. And it is this misunderstanding on their part that gives Jesus the excuse to make some pretty scathing comments of their persistent ability to miss the point.

But what *was* Jesus talking about when he spoke of yeast? The yeast he refers to is the yeast of the Pharisees and of Herod—an odd combination of parties who had little in common, beyond the fact that in their different ways each was a threat to Jesus and his preaching of the kingdom of God. Pharisees opposed him for theological reasons: he was preaching dangerously radical ideas and undermining their authority. Herod was afraid of what he had heard about him, as we have seen in 6:14–16, as a potential political danger, another populist leader like John the Baptist. But why 'yeast'?

Yeast was a traditional symbol for pervasive influence, sometimes good (Matthew 13:33), usually bad (1 Corinthians 5:6–9). It works unseen until the whole lump of dough is affected. The Pharisees and Herod in their different ways represent the insidious danger of a mistaken attitude to Jesus. Beware of being infected by it. That was probably what he intended the disciples to hear, but their preoccupation with their lack of bread prevented them from hearing it.

## Spiritual myopia

Jesus' language in verses 17–18 is extraordinarily strong. It reminds us of the ominous words from Isaiah which he used in 4:12. But there he was talking about 'outsiders', whereas the disciples were those to whom the secret had been revealed. But now it is the disciples themselves who are blind and deaf to the realities of the kingdom of God.

In particular, they have failed to learn the lesson of the two miracles of feeding. His careful reminder of the details of the two stories shows how important these two miracles were. So what is the lesson that they have failed to grasp? Is it that with Jesus in the boat they have no need to worry about lack of provisions? If so few loaves fed so many people with so much left over, surely one little roll is more than enough for a group of thirteen! Perhaps that is all he means, but perhaps also there is the more general criticism that they are still thinking of merely mundane matters when Jesus' mission is on a different level altogether. The feeding miracles did provide literal food indeed, but those who had experienced them ought surely also to be beginning to see that Jesus is more than just a provider of food. 'Do you not yet understand?'

### PRAYER

*Lord, we often fail to understand your purposes, and cannot see beyond our own little concerns. Please cure our blindness.*

# 52 A blind man cured— by stages

## Another healing outside Galilee

Bethsaida was across the Jordan at the north end of the lake, not in Galilee but in the neighbouring territory ruled by Herod Philip, adjoining the Decapolis. So this healing occurs in a similar area to that of 7:31–37, and it follows a similar pattern. In each case it is other people who approach Jesus on behalf of the sufferer, asking for a healing touch. In each Jesus deliberately withdraws from the public arena before healing, and then issues a command to silence. Each story goes into unusual detail on the actions performed by Jesus to effect the healing, each involving touching directly the affected organs, and the use of saliva.

## Blindness—literal and metaphorical

Act 2 of Mark's Gospel begins and ends with the healing of a blind man (see 10:45–52 for the second). In between Jesus will devote much of his attention to teaching his disciples, who will again and again show how little they have yet grasped of what Jesus' mission is all about. Their gradual awakening to the radical new dynamics of the kingdom of God is one of the main themes of this central section of the Gospel. So it is quite likely that Mark expected his readers to understand the two healings of blind men which frame the section not only literally but also symbolically. After all, Jesus has just described his disciples as spiritually blind (vv. 17–18). He has also called them deaf (v. 18), and we have seen that the healing of the deaf and dumb man in 7:31–37 is closely parallel to this story. So perhaps the two miracles are to be seen as a pair, important indeed in their literal sense, but also symbolic of the dawning of new understanding in the disciples.

# A two-stage healing

The story of the blind man at Bethsaida is unique in the Gospels in that when Jesus first lays his hands on the man's eyes the healing is only partial ('people like trees, walking') and it is only after a second touch that he sees everything clearly. Perhaps it is for this reason that neither Matthew nor Luke includes this story, as they may not have liked the suggestion that at first Jesus was not completely successful.

But Mark may have found it particularly appropriate to his purpose, since the restoration of 'sight' to the disciples also proceeded by stages. In 4:11 they were described as privileged to understand the secret of the kingdom of God, but by 8:17–18 they seem no better than the outsiders who cannot grasp the secret. In 8:29 Peter will make a great declaration of faith in Jesus as the Messiah, but three verses later he will reveal that he has still not grasped what Jesus' mission really involves. As the disciples struggle to come to terms with new realities in these three chapters, they will be like the blind man, seeing at first only dimly, and still needing further help to get things really clear.

## PRAYER

*Thy blessed unction from above*
*Is comfort, life, and fire of love;*
*Enable with perpetual light*
*The dullness of our blinded sight.*
**Veni Creator**

# 53 Peter declares his faith

Caesarea Philippi is the most northerly point of Jesus' journeys, in a remote non-Jewish area in the foothills of the Mount Hermon range. He takes his disciples not to the town itself but into the countryside, and the whole focus of this part of the story is on time spent by Jesus alone with his disciples. He has not come here for public ministry, but for private instruction. And like any good teacher he begins with questions.

## What do other people think?

He begins with the easier, more objective question. The disciples have no difficulty in reporting what they have gathered of popular opinion about Jesus. The answer is already familiar to us from 6:14–15, where the same three options (John the Baptist, Elijah, or an [unnamed] prophet) were being canvassed. We have thought about the names offered when we looked at that passage. All are variations on the theme 'prophet'. And as far as they go, they are right, for Jesus *is* a prophet, someone who speaks the word of God to the people of God, and calls them to respond to him.

But is that all there is to be said about Jesus? Is he merely a spokesman for God? And so we come to the second and much more searching question.

## What do *you* think?

It is typical of Peter that he emerges as the spokesman for the disciple group. They have been sharing together the extraordinary experiences of Jesus' teaching and miracles, and no doubt they have already been discussing together what they are to make of it all. It is unlikely that what Peter now says is a brand new idea thought up on the spur of the moment. But it is the first time the truth has been squarely faced, and it is Peter who has the honour, and the responsibility, of giving it open expression.

Jesus is the Messiah. The word would mean different things in detail to different groups of Jews, but to all of them it would have the ring of uniqueness and of finality. The one whose coming has long been foretold has at last arrived. The 'last days' of which the prophets have spoken are upon us. 'The time is fulfilled and the kingdom of God is at hand' (1:15).

So much would be agreed, but what does the coming of the kingdom of God mean? How is the Messiah to fulfil his pivotal role? Is he coming to bring spiritual renewal to God's people, or to deliver them from the sovereignty of Rome? It is here that there is too much room for misunderstanding, not to mention vested interests. The word 'Messiah' is a trigger for all sorts of different hopes and fears to be brought into play.

## The 'Messianic Secret'

Jesus' command to tell no-one must have been a terrible deflation after the euphoria which Peter's heady words would induce. But there is too much danger in unguarded talk of 'the Messiah' for Jesus to allow them to use it outside their own small circle. Even the disciples have a long way to go before they understand it themselves, as verses 31–33 will go on to show. So, for the time being, the secret must be kept. It will not be until 14:61–2, in very different circumstances, that Jesus lifts the embargo.

**PRAYER**

*Lord, give us the wisdom to know what may be said, and when, and to whom. Save us both from the timidity which will not speak and from unwisely blurting out what must be communicated with care.*

# 54 A dose of cold water

The command to maintain silence must have been deflating enough, but what follows is far harder to take.

## The martyrdom of the Son of man

The exciting title 'Messiah' is immediately dropped, and Jesus speaks of himself, as he usually does, as the 'Son of man'. This was a title without the ready-made associations of 'Messiah', and one which therefore Jesus could use to express what *he* wanted to say about his unique role, without the danger of triggering inappropriate hopes of political liberation.

But worse than the change of title is what Jesus actually says about his 'messianic' mission. It is the very opposite of what most Jews would have expected, and surely also of what Peter and the other disciples had in mind. Rather than being an all-conquering hero he is to be the victim of rejection and assassination. And worse still, those who reject and kill him are to be not the Romans (that would at least have been a noble if futile self-sacrifice), but the leaders of his own people. 'The elders, the chief priests, and the scribes' were the three groups who made up the Sanhedrin, the Jewish supreme court; you could not have a more formidable and authoritative listing of the Jewish authorities. And it is this Jewish power-group who will reject and eliminate Israel's Messiah!

## Peter gets it wrong

This is too much for Peter, fresh from the exhilaration of his great statement of faith. And the first part of verse 33 suggests that he is speaking also for the other disciples when he takes it upon himself to 'rebuke' Jesus. His protest is entirely natural—but that is just the trouble. He is speaking 'human thoughts', and completely missing the divine perspective. To human thinking a rejected and assassinated Messiah is sheer nonsense—but it is through such 'nonsense' that God's saving purpose is to be fulfilled (see Paul's comments in

1 Corinthians 1:18–25). To adopt this human perspective is to take the side of Satan.

## Take up your cross

And, still worse, it is not only Jesus who must face the cross, but his followers too. When they first responded to Jesus' 'Follow me' they can have had no idea of what this new commitment might involve, but now it is becoming painfully clear that they have joined not a triumphal procession but a funeral cortege. We have become so familiar with the language of 'taking up the cross' that we miss its stark and unpalatable meaning: the funeral is likely to be their own! To follow a martyr Messiah is to accept the risk of martyrdom.

So the shadow of the cross falls firmly across the road to Jerusalem, and several more times Jesus will remind them of it before they reach the capital, where the grim prediction will become only too real a fact. The cross is that of Jesus, but potentially it is also their own. Was this what they had reckoned with when they signed on as disciples of the Messiah?

### FOR MEDITATION

*Put yourself in the position of one of the twelve disciples, with all the experiences of chapters 1–8 behind you. How would you have reacted to Peter's confession and to Jesus' response to it? With what thoughts would you have set out on the road to Jerusalem? Would you have set out at all?*

113

# Ultimate realities

## Gaining and losing

Verses 35–37 are hard to translate, since the same Greek word, here translated by 'life' (but sometimes also by 'soul'), means both the fact of being physically alive and not dead and also the real self which is far more than physical life and which survives beyond it. Jesus' words depend on the contrast between these two senses of the same Greek word. To cling to (physical) life may be to forfeit (spiritual) life, while those who lose their (physical) life because of their loyalty to the cause of the gospel will find that their true (spiritual) life is saved and not lost. The ultimate question, then, is which is more worth preserving. In the light of his command to 'take up the cross' it is a real and pressing question for the disciples as they set out for Jerusalem.

## A choice of loyalty

The language about the Son of man 'coming' in glory and in the company of angels is a clear echo of the vision of Daniel 7:13–14, the passage from which Jesus drew his chosen title 'the Son of man'. In that vision the 'one like a son of man' comes before God and is given eternal and universal sovereignty over all nations. It is a heavenly enthronement scene, and is set in a context of universal judgment. So the same 'Son of man' who will die in Jerusalem is destined after that to be enthroned as judge of all people.

To recognize this will put the disciples' choice in a new perspective. To fail under the more immediate pressure of human opposition is to risk the more ultimate danger of being repudiated by the Judge of all, whom they have chosen to follow and then have denied. When you put it like that, who would want to throw in their lot with 'this adulterous and sinful generation'?

# Seeing and believing

Some of those who have taken up their cross to follow the Son of man may well have to 'taste death' before they see any fruition for their loyalty in this life. For them it will be only the ultimate encounter with the Son of man after death which will vindicate their loyalty. But for others there will be something to show for their faithfulness even in this life: they 'will see that the kingdom of God has come with power'.

Jesus does not say when and how they will see it, and interpreters have offered many guesses. There is no reason to imagine that he was referring to his second coming: that is not what he says. Perhaps the kingdom of God will be seen to have come in power in Jesus' own vindication by resurrection after his death; perhaps in his visible ascension to the right hand of power; perhaps in the coming of the Holy Spirit, or in the powerful spread of the gospel among the nations in the decades after Pentecost. Certainly while some of those first disciples were still alive there would be ample evidence, for those with the eyes to see it, that the kingdom of God, planted secretly like a little mustard seed, was now beginning its growth into a great bush. The authority of the Son of Man enthroned at God's right hand would soon be seen in its power and glory.

### PRAYER

*Lord, you know how strongly we are affected by the people and pressures which surround us. Help us to see beyond the immediate, to have the eyes to see the evidence of your power at work in our world, and to see beyond this world to your ultimate power and glory. And so may our loyalty be rightly placed, where it will matter in the end.*

# 56 The veil is drawn aside

There is a further possible meaning of Jesus' puzzling saying in verse 1 about seeing that the kingdom of God has come with power. For 'some' (only three) of those who heard it would indeed have a more immediate vision of power and glory, a foretaste of what was to come after Jesus' death and resurrection. Mark does not usually link his episodes together with careful notes of time, and perhaps the unusual precision here ('after six days') is meant to alert us to the link between verse 1 and the incident which follows so closely upon it.

## A vision of glory

Mark relates this extraordinary vision from the point of view of the three disciples who were privileged to witness it, speaking throughout of what *they* saw, experienced, heard and felt. After the depressing words at the end of chapter 8 no doubt they needed some encouragement to offset the gloom which must have descended on the disciple group. But this was more than just a timely reassurance. It lifted their understanding of Jesus to new and amazing heights.

We have no way of knowing how such a 'vision' (as Matthew calls it, Matthew 17:9) came about, whether there was anything which a cine-camera could have recorded, or whether it was 'all in the mind'. But Mark records it as a shared experience which seemed to Peter real enough to make him think of building physical dwellings for the visionary visitors.

There is no other story like this in the Gospels. Jesus' power and authority as the Son of God is displayed in many ways, but always in the form of what appears to be an ordinary human being. But here the veil is briefly drawn aside, and the glory of heaven shines through. No wonder they are bewildered and frightened as they see the dazzling light and Jesus recognizable and yet transformed. Then, just as Jesus had after his baptism (1:11) they hear the voice of God himself identifying Jesus as his Son. In 1:11 God spoke to Jesus himself, but now he speaks to the disciples and calls them to accept his authority and 'listen to him'. After this there can be no choice as to whom they are to follow, whatever the cost.

## Elijah and Moses

Elijah and Moses have been long dead, yet here they are 'talking with Jesus'! Elijah, as we have seen, was expected to come back to usher in the Day of the Lord, and Moses had left a promise that God would send to his people 'a prophet like me' (Deuteronomy 18:15). So the reappearance of these two worthies from Israel's past marks the time for the fulfilment of God's promises. Moreover, there are other links between these two men and the story of Jesus. Both were men sent by God but rejected by his people. Both had to battle with loneliness and misunderstanding. Both had gone up on a high mountain to meet with God. And these two men, together with Enoch, were famous as the three who had mysteriously disappeared from the earth, Elijah in a chariot of fire and Moses on a mountain where 'no one knows his burial place' (Deuteronomy 34:6).

Peter, James and John probably understood little of this at the time. Peter's strange proposal to erect impromptu shelters on the mountain is perhaps a clumsy attempt to do justice to the presence of such august visitors. Perhaps too he has hopes of 'fixing' this passing experience in physical structures, but if so he is unsuccessful, because soon the whole mind-blowing experience is over. and nothing remains but the memory.

**PRAYER**

*Thank you, Lord, for the 'mountain-top' experiences you sometimes allow us to enjoy. Help us to draw strength from them, but not to cling to them, and to know the reality of Jesus' divine glory and authority in the valley as well.*

# 57
# What about Elijah?

There is something bizarre and yet reassuring in the picture of Jesus walking down the mountain in earnest conversation with Peter, James and John, so soon after they have seen him bathed in dazzling light and talking with men long dead. The otherworldly vision is over, and now they must return to ordinary life. But what they have seen on the mountain has left them with a lot to think about.

## Sworn to secrecy

Can you imagine how Peter, James and John would have enjoyed telling their story to the others—and what the others might have made of it? But they are not to have the opportunity. If Peter's declaration that Jesus is the Messiah has had to be embargoed, how much more this vision of him as the Son of God. This was not to be a matter of public amazement and speculation. It was 'for their eyes only'.

But this time there is a time limit. The embargo remains 'until after the Son of man has risen from the dead'. When Jesus talked in 8:31 of his forthcoming death, he had also predicted that he would rise again after three days. The disciples clearly can make nothing of such language, and even after three more such predictions (9:31; 10:34; 14:28) they will still be caught unawares by his physical resurrection.

## 'Elijah has come'

But for now they have another matter on their minds. When they saw Elijah on the mountain they began to put the pieces together, and realized that this had something to do with the coming of the last days. But how does it all fit? Are the scribes right that Elijah must come first? If so, where is he? Was this vision perhaps all that his promised coming would amount to? Or is he still waiting in the wings?

Yes, says Jesus, the scribes are right (and indeed it was not their idea: they got it from Malachi 4:5–6!). But what they and the disciples have failed to realize is that that prophecy has already been fulfilled, in the coming of John the Baptist as the 'Elijah' of the last days (see comments on his Elijah-image, on 1:4–8). Not that Jesus names John the Baptist here, but the reference to what 'they did to him' is a clear allusion to the story of the death of John which Mark has told in 6:17–29. And in John's fate Jesus sees a foreshadowing of his own: if 'Elijah' has been treated like that, surely the Son of man must expect no better response. He too must 'go through many sufferings and be treated with contempt'.

So even on the way down from the mountain of glory the shadow of the cross still falls. The Son of God who has shone on the mountain is the same as the Son of man who will suffer on the cross, but who will also rise from the dead. Is it any wonder that the disciples are finding it all too hard to grasp?

## PRAYER

*Lord, help us to grasp as much as you want us to grasp of your truth, and to trust you where we do not yet understand.*

# 58 Why the disciples failed

After the splendour of the mountain top comes a sad contrast, a story of human distress and of the failure of faith. This will be the last time Mark tells of an exorcism by Jesus, but he tells this story as much to explain why the disciples failed to help the possessed boy as to display yet again Jesus' total mastery over the powers of evil. It is a lesson about faith and prayer rather than just another miracle of Jesus.

## Demon-possession and physical illness

We have noted repeatedly that Mark uses different language for demon-possession and exorcism from that which he uses for physical illness and its cure. The two are different situations, and are not to be confused. But the vivid description of the physical suffering of the boy in this story (vv. 18, 20, 22) is so similar to what we know as an epileptic fit that it is often rather unthinkingly referred to as the story of 'The epileptic boy'.

There is no doubt that Mark understands it as a case of demon-possession, both in his description of the problem and in the way Jesus confronts and expels the unclean spirit in verses 25–26. Our knowledge of ancient medical thinking is not full enough for us to say how widely epilepsy (sometimes known in pagan circles as 'the divine illness') was taken to be a spiritual rather than a purely physical affliction. Knowledge of brain function was very limited, and it would be quite understandable if the symptoms of epilepsy were attributed to a supernatural force. But Mark does not use any word meaning 'epilepsy', and we are on safer ground if we take it to be, as Mark describes it, a case of demon-possession which had severe physical and behavioural repercussions.

## The disciples' failure

While Jesus and the three disciples have been away the rest of the group have found themselves confronted by a situation which they could not cope with. When Jesus had sent them out in 6:7 their commission was specifically to have 'authority over the unclean spirits' and they were then able to 'cast out many demons' (6:13) without having Jesus with them. So why have they not been able to do the same now? Was that authority given them only for the specific occasion of the mission in chapter 6? There is no indication that this was so. Or was there something uniquely demanding about this particular case which lifted it out of the normal run of exorcisms? Both symptoms and exorcism are indeed described in unusually lurid detail, but it is not easy to see why one demon should be more resistant to the delegated authority of Jesus than another.

The disciples themselves are taken by surprise: 'Why could we not cast it out?' Jesus' reply is equally surprising. He does not specify what 'this kind' are, but it is strange that prayer is the key to 'this kind' rather than to all exorcisms, and even more strange that he implies that the disciples had *not* in fact prayed about this case. One might have expected that to be normal.

## Faith and prayer

So is the point perhaps that after their earlier successes they have become blasé, and have assumed that they have been given an automatic guarantee of success, instead of turning to God for the authority which is needed in this (and every) case? Those who have been for some time in Christian ministry are too easily prone to taking God's work for granted. The whole story is thus a salutary reminder that there is nothing automatic about spiritual conflict. Even the twelve must depend not on their status as Jesus' chosen agents but on the power which comes through prayer.

The key word again is 'faith'. It is 'faithlessness' that Jesus complains of (v. 19), and 'faith' which is the essential condition of deliverance (vv. 23–24). It is the faith of the disciples which has proved inadequate, as they have failed to pray.

### PRAYER
*'Lord, I believe. Help my unbelief!'*

# 59 Another warning of what is to come

In this brief paragraph we find several of the key themes which run through the middle section (Act 2) of Mark's story, as Jesus and his disciples make their way from Galilee towards Jerusalem. We may therefore take it as an opportunity to remind ourselves of how the drama is developing.

## Private teaching

Jesus' attempts to avoid public notice have been a repeated feature of the story ever since chapter 1. But this time we are given the reason for it. It is because he is teaching his disciples. During the time in Galilee the disciples have learned along with the crowds, with further private explanation added from time to time. But now the time has come to focus down more narrowly on the little group who will be the key to the continuation of Jesus' mission when he himself is no longer there. So in Act 2 there is relatively little public activity, and Jesus and his disciples travel together as a small group. And as they go, he teaches them many things to do with the kingdom of God. They have many new things to grasp while he is still there to teach them, and the time is short.

## The shadow of the cross

The shock statement with which Jesus has launched the journey towards Jerusalem in 8:31 is repeated here and again in more detail in 10:33–34. This awful new dimension to their understanding of Jesus' mission is thus relentlessly kept before their reluctant minds. The heady days of public acclaim and popularity in Galilee are over, and Jesus is on his way to martyrdom. And that means that it will not be very long before they must learn to manage without him. But above all they must learn to recognize that the death which he so unequivocally predicts is not to be an unfortunate accident, but is the very goal of his ministry. What it will achieve is so far left unexplained, though later he will spell it out for them (10:45; 14:22–25). And again there is that tantalizing hint that for Jesus death will not be the end, but he will rise again after three days. All this is so new, and so stunning, that even with constant repetition it will take them all their time even to begin to grasp it.

## 'They did not understand'

Already Jesus has complained at the disciples' failure to understand (8:17–21). This failure is a repeated theme of these chapters. Immediately after each of the three predictions of his death we come down to earth with a bump as the disciples reveal in various ways their complete lack of sympathy with the new values of the kingdom of God (8:32; 9:33–34; 10:35–37). And each time Jesus patiently (or not so patiently, 8:33!) puts them right.

Everything is so new and unexpected, and so contrary to conventional human thinking, that it needs a complete programme of re-education to accustom the disciples to the radical and paradoxical values of the kingdom of God. And much of it they would rather not learn. The little note in verse 32 that 'they were afraid to ask him' indicates not so much that Jesus was difficult to approach, but rather that they had enough of an inkling of what he was talking about to know that they would rather not hear it spelled out!

**PRAYER**

*Lord, be patient with our slowness to grasp your truth, and lead us on to new understanding. And when you need to teach us things we would rather not hear, give us the courage to face up to them.*

123

# 60 Who is the greatest?

## Lines of authority

In a newly formed group of colleagues with an important task, it is natural to want to clarify the lines of authority. So far, of course, Jesus has been the focal authority of the group, but if they are going to lose him it will surely be vital to establish a clear pecking order. So they feel the need to decide between themselves 'who is the greatest?'. Any management consultant would have urged them to do so.

The issue comes up repeatedly in the Gospels, and will be tackled more fully in 10:35–45. But already it seems that the disciples are beginning to be aware that Jesus looks at this question of status rather differently. When he wants to know what they have been talking about, they refuse to reply—for all the world like a group of naughty schoolboys who have been caught misbehaving by the teacher.

## Greatness in service

'The first will be last' was something of a slogan of Jesus' teaching. It will be stated more definitively in 10:31, and its implications for leadership in the disciple group will be spelled out more fully in 10:42–45. Here it is stated with devastating simplicity. Rather than looking for greatness, they should be eager to be at the bottom of the pile. Rather than aiming to dominate others, they should aspire to be the servant of all. The object of their ambition should be not influence and authority but usefulness. The greatest is the least and the leader is the dogsbody.

That is not the way most people think. Such an attitude is not even respected. It is not noble but demeaning. The people who get things done are the aggressive and ruthless, and people respect the leadership of those who assert themselves. Jesus' upside-down principle of greatness would be dismissed by most people, then and now, as at best whimsical and unrealistic.

# The example of a child

Jesus, good teacher as he is, reinforces his startling pronouncement with a visual aid. The child symbolizes the 'least'. Children are at the bottom of the authority structure of society. They are expected to do as they are told, and have no self-determination. They are to be looked after, not to be looked up to. They are all too easily over-looked and exploited by adult society. And they long for the day when they in their turn will be grown up and able to tell others what to do.

But for Jesus the child represents the one who matters in the kingdom of God. Anyone who wants to share the values of Jesus must welcome and respect the little one as much as (or more than?) the great. The last are to be first. For behind the vulnerable figure of the child stands Jesus himself, and behind Jesus stands 'the one who sent me'. Remember Jesus' words in Matthew 25:40: 'Just as you did it to one of the least of these... you did it to me'.

## FOR MEDITATION

*In what ways should we as followers of Jesus challenge the accepted ideas of our society about status and leadership? How far are we ourselves conditioned by the assumption that 'the first shall be first'?*

# 61 'Not one of us'

John the son of Zebedee was one of the 'Sons of Thunder' (3:17) and here he lives up to his name. In 10:35–40 he and his brother James will show even more blatantly how far they have yet to go to grasp the values of the kingdom of God.

## Building barriers, not bridges

The issue here is cliquishness. It is natural for most groups of people to develop a sense of group identity, and to erect barriers to define who does and who does not belong. And for a religious group, whose concern is properly with truth and orthodoxy, this is an even more natural tendency. The history of religion is all too often the history of drawing lines of demarcation, of secessions and expulsions, of schism and of closing ranks. It is characteristic of many religious people to be sure that 'I am right and you are wrong', and to insist that 'what is not done my way should not be done at all'.

So it was natural for John to conclude that a man who was casting out demons (apparently successfully) but did not belong to the disciple group, was not to be tolerated. He was using Jesus' name, but was not one of Jesus' disciples. He was at best a fellow-traveller, at worst a charlatan. But in any case he was 'not one of us'.

## A more welcoming approach

The existence of such a character need not surprise us. Exorcism was a recognized (if not widespread) practice among the Jews. Jesus refers to other Jewish exorcists apparently with approval in Matthew 12:27, and we meet others in Acts 19:13–16. And Jesus will not allow John to write this man off. Whatever his background, he is engaged in good work. He is on the side of good against evil.

Jesus reinforces this open attitude with a series of comments in verses 39–41 on the approach to people who are 'not one of us'. The disciple group may find support from unexpected quarters, and they should welcome and not repel it. There are people out there who may not themselves wear the name of Christ on their sleeve, but who in the end will prove to be supporters and not opponents. Such people 'will by no means lose their reward'.

## For or against

The refreshingly open-minded attitude of this section is summed up in the formula: 'Whoever is not against us is for us'. John would no doubt have preferred to invoke the saying in Matthew 12:30 (again in a context of exorcism), 'Whoever is not with me is against me'. On either formula there is no room for neutrality, but what a difference of atmosphere between the open, welcoming attitude of this verse and the exclusivism of the other. In different circumstances there may be a place for either, but we should beware of the natural tendency to jump to the negative conclusion when faced with an 'outsider' who may in fact turn out to be 'for' rather than 'against'.

**PRAYER**

*Thank you, Lord, that you welcome us. Help us to welcome others in your name.*

# 62
# Hard sayings

These verses contain a collection of sayings, probably originally independent of each other, which are linked by 'catch-words': stumbling, fire, salt. They draw out some of the demands and the perils of discipleship, and warn against an easy, lax approach which refuses to take the kingdom of God seriously.

## Verse 42

The child of verses 36–37 and the donor of the cup of water in verse 41 are examples of the 'little ones' whom a careless disciple may cause to stumble. Such people are easily ignored or pushed aside. But if a disciple's attitude or actions makes it harder for them to find their place in the kingdom of God, that is a serious matter, so serious that even drowning would be better than the fate which such behaviour deserves.

## Verses 43–48

But 'stumbling' may be caused not only by someone else but by something in our own lives. The disciple who is 'tripped up' by his or her own hand, foot or eye would be better off without the offending part of the body. The hand, foot and eye are probably to be taken as symbolic of areas of personality or behaviour which may prevent us from fulfilling our calling as disciples. Bad habits and bad company may make it impossible for us to live the life of the kingdom of God. If that is the case, let them be cut out before it is too late. The alternative is hell, 'Gehenna', the name of the rubbish tip outside Jerusalem where refuse was thrown out and burned. The chilling words 'their worm never dies and the fire is not quenched', drawing on the picture of the rubbish tip, make it luridly clear how much is at stake. Here is Jesus at his most severe, an important corrective to the 'cuddly' image of Jesus which is sometimes presented.

# Verse 49

This verse is a puzzle. Perhaps it draws on the Old Testament ritual in which salt was added to sacrifices, and so pictures the disciple as a living sacrifice to God. Or perhaps it suggests that fire which can destroy (as in verses 43–48) can also be used to purify and preserve, as salt does, so that a disciple's painful experience may bring salvation in the end. But it remains obscure.

# Verse 50

Here are two more sayings involving salt. Salt was used by the rabbis as a metaphor for wisdom, and Paul uses it similarly in Colossians 4:5–6. A disciple's life and words should contribute to the 'flavour' of life by their wisdom and suitability. But if we lose our Christian distinctiveness the 'salt' goes out of our discipleship, and we cease to be of any value to those around us. A life without Christian wisdom is as unpalatable, and as liable to go bad, as food without salt. But where Christian 'saltiness' is maintained, it will avoid conflict and promote peace with one another.

A strange and rather incoherent section of the Gospel, but one which is full of provocative nuggets of thought by which we can test the seriousness and effectiveness of our own discipleship.

## PRAYER

*Lord, save us from the casual and uncaring approach to the kingdom of God which puts our own and other people's discipleship at risk.*

# 63 No place for divorce

## Divorce—now and then

In a society in which divorce has become normal and accepted, Jesus' robust condemnation of it comes as a shock. But the same was true in his own day. While Jewish authorities debated the grounds for divorce, no-one questioned that divorce as such was permissible. After all, had not Moses given explicit directions to regulate it (Deuteronomy 24:1-4)? Some taught that the 'something objectionable' mentioned in Deuteronomy 24:1 meant adultery and nothing more, while others (and their view was inevitably the more popular among Jewish men) taught that it could cover even quite trivial matters like bad cooking or even not being pretty enough. The casual approach that prevailed is summed up in Josephus' laconic comment in his autobiography: 'At this time I divorced my wife, since I did not like her behaviour.' The main difference from our own situation was that in Jewish law a man could divorce his wife with a minimum of fuss, but the woman could not divorce her husband.

## Going back to first principles

Jesus' first response to the question is to establish the legal basis for divorce in the Old Testament. There is only one relevant legal text, and that is the one they quote. But in fact they do not quote it exactly, since Deuteronomy 24:1-4 does not in fact explicitly 'allow divorce', but rather regulates what may and may not happen once a divorce has been officially recognized and the woman has remarried. Moses certainly *assumes* divorce, and it may be argued that this implies that he 'allows' it. That was the basis on which the whole Jewish approach to divorce rested. But it would be going too far to claim that Moses either commanded or approved divorce; he merely regulated the aftermath. That is what Jesus means by describing his regulations as 'because of the hardness of your hearts'—they were a concession to human weakness, not a statement of the way things ought to have been.

So Jesus turns their attention instead not to the concession but to the original statement of God's intention for marriage in the first two chapters of Genesis. The key concept is that a man and a woman form 'one flesh', by entering into a new and exclusive union in place of their previous parental links. Marriage, in other words, is not just a contract for mutual convenience (and therefore able to be terminated when it ceases to suit the parties), but the creation of a new and indivisible unit of man and woman as 'one flesh'.

## Marriage is for ever

If that is how God intended marriage to be, it is not for human beings to tamper with it. 'What God has joined together, let no one separate.' There it is, God's standard for marriage stated simply, clearly, unequivocally, and without a hint of any basis for divorce. Divorce is, quite simply, against the will of God.

The boldness of Jesus' statement is breathtaking. In Matthew's version (5:32; 19:9) there is an escape clause, 'except on the ground of unchastity', but in Mark and Luke (16:18) it is entirely unqualified. In the next study we shall return to the question of how we are to live with this absolute demand in the real world, and of how the standard set out in Genesis relates to the concession allowed in Deuteronomy, but for now it is important that we do not seek to evade the uncompromising call to lifelong fidelity in marriage. The moment we begin to think about exceptions and concessions (and, as Matthew's 'escape clause' reminds us, we cannot avoid doing so in dealing with real people in a real world), this simple clarity is lost, and we are in danger of treating as normal what is in fact the betrayal of God's plan for marriage. Jesus insists instead that we go back to the way God meant it to be, and draw our standards from there.

**PRAYER**

*Forgive us, Lord, for our eagerness to find the easy way out, and our fear of facing up to your full demand. Restore to us and to our society the vision of marriage as you meant it to be.*

# 64

# Did Jesus really mean it?

As in 7:17 and in chapter 4 a startling pronouncement is followed by the disciples asking Jesus to explain it. Surely he could not really want to sweep away the whole possibility of divorce (which Moses apparently allowed) at one go? So what did he mean?

## Divorce and remarriage

But the explanation which follows in no way weakens the demand made in verse 9. Rather it spells out in more practical detail what are its radical implications. Divorce followed by remarriage is tantamount to adultery since it violates the 'one flesh' union. If the divorce was not permissible, clearly neither is the remarriage: you cannot be married to two people at once.

It is sometimes suggested that Jesus' words apply only to the remarriage which follows on a divorce, and that Jesus does not condemn a divorce if the parties then remain unmarried. In terms of the precise words of verses 11–12 this is a possible interpretation, but it flies in the face of the absolute prohibition of divorce in verse 9, where the issue of remarriage had not yet been raised. In any case, in Jewish society at the time it would have made no sense to talk of divorce without the right to remarry: divorce was precisely the setting free of a formerly married person to marry again. So it is not the remarriage as such which is the focus of Jesus' condemnation, but the breaking of the one-flesh union, whether or not another marriage follows.

(Mark, alone among the Gospels, envisages in verse 12 a wife divorcing her husband as well as vice versa. While this was impossible in Jewish law it was allowed in Roman law, and Mark, if he was writing in Rome, may have included this logical extension of the principle for the sake of those around him.)

# Biblical ideals in the real world

Mark therefore offers us an unqualified and total rejection of divorce by Jesus. Marriage is 'till death us do part'. But divorces do in fact happen, and Moses had already provided legislation to deal with what follows from a divorce. Are we then to say that Moses was wrong even to countenance the possibility? According to Jesus he provided for divorce 'because of your hardness of heart'—and human hearts are still hard, and marriages do break down. Should those who follow Jesus simply close their eyes to this reality? Or should they sadly accept that Jesus' ideal teaching, wonderful as it is, simply does not fit the way things are?

There is a way between these two extremes, but it is a difficult one to define and to practise without inconsistency. It is to insist *both* that God's standard is absolute and that divorce can never be good, *and also* that in a world which is characterized by human weakness and failure it must be possible to find ways of coping with a broken marriage (as Moses found that he had to). In that case divorce and remarriage, while it can never be good, may be the least bad of the options available. It may thus be the right thing to do in the circumstances, but can never cease to be a cause for regret and sorrow that God's standard for marriage has been violated. Perhaps it is this reluctant recognition of the realities of human failure which led Matthew to include his clause allowing divorce in the case of 'unchastity'.

But if, reluctantly, we come to this conclusion, it is a very different matter from accepting the verdict of society that divorce is 'OK', and assuming that Jesus' words are an unworkable ideal. They are not. They are the way God expects marriage to be, and woe betide the church and society once that clear standard is allowed to fade into only an unreachable ideal. Divorce and remarriage can never be more than the outworking of human weakness, a recognition of failure.

## FOR MEDITATION

*How has it been possible for society to move so far from the clear teaching of Jesus, and how can the church now both witness to God's purpose for marriage and also offer appropriate pastoral help to those whose marriages are in trouble?*

# 65 Whose is the kingdom of God?

The 'kingdom of God' is mentioned twice in these verses, and three times more in verses 23–25. The phrase, as we have seen, means 'God's rule', and what the disciples are being forced to face in this series of incidents are some of the radically different ways in which life must be lived under God's sovereignty as compared with the conventions of human society. The programme of re-education for the disciples which has been under way since Caesarea Philippi is now coming to its climax as Jesus draws nearer to Jerusalem, and one blow after another to the disciples' unthinking assumptions leaves them, and us, reeling before the values of the kingdom of God which seem to turn all our natural expectations upside down.

## Do not stop them

It was the custom for children to be brought to the elders for blessing on the Day of Atonement, and perhaps that was the occasion for this incident. Or perhaps this was something less formal: people wanted Jesus to touch and bless their children, just as they wanted him to heal those who were ill.

But the disciples are not happy with this. Perhaps they feel that it is beneath the master's dignity to be worried with children, or perhaps, aware of the great threats hanging over Jesus, they want to protect him being troubled and distracted by lesser concerns. Jesus has better things to do than to be stopping to bless children.

After the lesson the disciples have already been taught in 9:36–37 you would think they would have a clearer understanding of Jesus' sense of priorities, but old prejudices die hard, and for the adult male children are not a priority. So again (they must be getting used to this!) they get a good telling off from Jesus, and once again he proceeds to turn their values upside down.

# Children and the kingdom of God

Jesus makes two separate comments relating to children and the kingdom of God.

First, the kingdom of God belongs to 'such as these'. In the light of 9:33–37 we are probably right not to take this as referring exclusively, or even mainly, to children as such. 'Such as these' means rather those in the childlike position, the weak, vulnerable, unnoticed members of society, the people who are easily marginalized by a macho disciple, the 'little ones' of 9:42. Not that this excludes children, of course; it was because they were keeping actual children away from him that Jesus said it. But it is wider than that. The kingdom of God 'belongs to' such people in the sense that they are the ones who most naturally fit into it. The God who 'has brought down the powerful from their thrones and lifted up the lowly' (Luke 1:52) rejoices to have such people as his subjects, and it is from them, not from the self-important, that we can best learn how to serve him.

Secondly, in order to enter God's kingdom, to become his true subjects, we must receive it 'as a little child'. The child is dependent, and knows it. What the child receives from grown-ups is not earned or fought for. The child's empty hand receives simply and gratefully. That is how we must receive God's kingship and the blessings it brings to those who know they cannot deserve his grace, but simply enjoy it.

## PRAYER

*Lord, make us more like children in our relationship with you,
and more ready to welcome and value those whom society does not
regard as important.*

# 66 A potential disciple lost

## The man who had everything

From the disciples' point of view this man must have seemed the ideal recruit. He was an earnest seeker for eternal life, with a good moral record (v. 20). According to Matthew he was a young man, and according to Luke a ruler. And he was very rich. Any religious movement would go to great lengths to gain such an adherent, and here he was making contact of his own accord. If ever there was a case for the red-carpet treatment, this must be it.

But instead Jesus sends him away with his tail between his legs. Whatever can he be thinking of? What is the kingdom of God all about if it is not interested in such a recruit as this? We shall consider the disciples' amazed reaction in the next study, but first we must listen to the dialogue between Jesus and the rich enquirer.

## What is 'good'?

His address to Jesus as 'Good Teacher' is probably mere politeness, but Jesus takes it as an opportunity to raise a fundamental issue. The man's opening question seems to assume that eternal life is to be 'earned' by doing good things. Like many people today, he perhaps thinks of salvation as rather like sitting an examination, and coming up with high enough marks to pass. Jesus' unexpected response turns the spotlight away from doing good things to the one true focus of goodness, which is in God himself. (To read Jesus' words, as some do, as implying that he himself is not good and therefore is not God is to take them completely out of context. The discussion is about eternal life, not about who Jesus is.)

Jesus first offers him the ten commandments (or rather that part of them which relates to how we treat other people, without the commandments touching on our relationship with God). But this is all familiar ground, and if that was all the man wanted to be told he would not have come to Jesus with his urgent question. Despite his (no doubt sincere) claim to have kept the commandments, he is not satisfied: there must be something more. Jesus may well have been hoping for such a response, as it shows that the man is aware of a dimension to salvation which is more than just keeping rules. So far, so good, and the comment that Jesus 'loved him' suggests that his response has struck the right note; he is ready for the 'something more'.

## Sell and give; come and follow

The 'one thing lacking' is a bombshell. It cuts away the whole basis of the man's life and status, his reputation and his security. Jesus' searching demand penetrates his defences and exposes where his priorities really lie. He is not ready for the kingdom of God.

Which of us would have done any better? Of course preachers are usually careful to point out (rightly) that Jesus does not seem to have demanded such a radical renunciation of all his disciples, and many have gratefully concluded that this man must have had a particular problem with money, and that Jesus would not say the same to the rest of us who (we trust) are not tempted in the same way. If that is what you think, here are some wise words from a commentator: 'That Jesus did not command all his followers to sell all their possessions gives comfort only to the kind of people to whom he *would* issue that command.'

We hear no more about this rich man. We may wonder whether he ever did find his way to eternal life.

#### PRAYER

*Lord, most of us play at being disciples for most of the time. Help us to face up to what following you really means for us, and to put first things first.*

# 67 No hope for the rich?

## The eye of a needle

The disciples are shocked, and Jesus does nothing to soothe their feelings, but rather makes things worse by the stark statement, twice repeated, that the way into the kingdom of God is hard for the wealthy. In a society which regarded affluence as a sign of God's blessing, this was crazy talk. And then, to make matters worse, Jesus says that it is not only hard, but impossible—unless, that is, a camel really can go through the eye of a needle!

Some commentators, in a misguided attempt to turn the impossible into the extraordinarily difficult, have suggested that 'the eye of a needle' was the name of a small door through which it might be just possible to envisage a camel being squeezed if it offloaded all its baggage. There is no evidence to support this nineteenth-century notion, and it has the effect both of destroying Jesus' proverbial image (the rabbis also used an elephant going through the eye of a needle as a figure for what is totally impossible) and of making nonsense of the disciples' reply. They at least understood Jesus to mean what he said, that it was impossible.

By human standards it is indeed impossible: the conflict between God and Mammon for our loyalty is a deadly one. But dealing with the impossible is God's speciality. Take it out of the realm of human endeavour, and there is hope after all. For what Jesus is talking about is the kingdom *of God* (the phrase is repeated three times to make sure we don't miss it), and in the kingdom of God everything is the other way up, and the impossible is possible.

## Losses and gains

Peter's comment in verse 28 sounds very smug: 'At least *we* are all right!' But Jesus takes him quite seriously. Yes, true discipleship has meant for them, as it would have meant for the rich man, the loss of material security. But no-one who puts the kingdom of God first will in the end be a loser. There will be recompense on a grand scale, not only in the age to come, but even here in this age. The experience of becoming a member of the new family (remember 3:31–35?) will compensate a hundredfold for all that has been forfeited.

But there are two stings in the tail. The first is the word 'persecutions', slipped in at the end of the list of earthly gains; it is not all joy for the disciple. The second is the formula about the first being last and the last first. It would be possible to take these words as simply a positive statement of the disciples' privilege: by making themselves 'last' they have in fact become 'first', while those like the rich man who have clung to their status have become the last. But in view of the discussions about precedence within the disciple group which we have already seen (9:33–35) and will soon meet in a yet sharper form (10:35–45), it may well be that this is also a gentle rebuke to Peter: 'Yes, you have done well to give up so much for me, but don't imagine that even that now guarantees you the top rank in the kingdom of God!'

## FOR MEDITATION

*'Many who are first will be last, and the last will be first.' In what ways can this slogan be seen as summing up the lessons learned by the disciples in the last couple of chapters? And how should it apply to our own attitudes in relation to the values of the kingdom of God?*

# 68 The death march

## 'Were you there ..?'

Verse 32 is one of the most vivid pieces of descriptive writing in Mark's Gospel, and seems to preserve the impression of someone who was there at the time, who was himself part of the tableau this verse presents. Peter seems the most obvious candidate.

The scene is 'on the road', a phrase which has become a familiar theme in this part of the Gospel with its restless onward movement (8:27; 9:33; 10:17; 10:52). The goal is Jerusalem, now directly named in verses 32 and 33 (it was there only by implication in 8:31 and 9:31)—and we already know from 3:22 and 7:1 what sort of reception Jesus can expect in Jerusalem. Yet for all that Mark allows us to see Jesus striding purposefully ahead on the road, leading the way impatiently towards what he knows is his own death. But his eagerness is not shared by his disciples, who are perhaps slowly beginning to realize that he means what he has said about what lies ahead. They follow him 'amazed', while an apparently larger group of fellow-travellers are quite simply 'afraid'. The contrast between the determined leader and the reluctant followers is striking, the more so when we remember that it is *his* death, not theirs, which is the immediate prospect.

## A third prediction of what lies ahead

And so we come to the third of Jesus' direct predictions of what is to happen when they get to Jerusalem. It agrees with the others, but this time he goes into more detail. His death is to follow an official trial and condemnation, and to the death itself are now added the shame and humiliation of the mocking, spitting and flogging which will precede it. Jesus is fully aware of the horror which lies ahead, and does not want his disciples to be taken by surprise when it all happens.

And yet Jesus again describes himself by the majestic title 'the Son of man', the figure who in Daniel 7:13-14 is destined to receive the homage of all people and to rule over the whole world for ever. The paradox of using such a title to speak of such abuse and suffering is extraordinary, and lends added pathos to his words.

This time there is also a further note added, that Jesus' condemnation and death, while it will begin with the Jewish authorities (the chief priests and scribes) will also involve the Gentiles, the Roman occupying forces in whose hands the death penalty officially rests. It is not clear whether the mocking, spitting, flogging and killing are to be understood here as the action of the Jewish leaders or of the Gentiles, but in the event it will make little difference, since both groups will be equally involved (14:65–66; 15:15–20).

But at the end of this terrible litany of suffering and rejection comes again the simple, unexplained note, 'after three days he will rise again'. To those who understand, it makes all the difference, but to the disciples at the time it probably remained a puzzle, as it had been in 9:10.

## PRAYER

*Lord, sometimes to follow where you lead is a bewildering and frightening business. Even when we are afraid help us still to follow, as your disciples did on the road to Jerusalem.*

*69*

# An inappropriate request

The two 'Sons of Thunder' (3:17) have appeared from time to time along with Peter as the small group with whom alone Jesus has shared and will share some of his most private moments (1:29; 5:37; 9:2; 14:33). The three of them with Andrew were the first disciples called to follow Jesus (1:16–20), and they are mentioned together at the head of the list of the twelve in 3:16–17. So they can reasonably think of themselves as leaders in the group. But it has been Peter who has taken the lead and acted as spokesman for the group on several occasions. James and John may well have begun to feel over-shadowed, and decided that it was time to assert their position. Hence this bizarre approach to Jesus.

## Sitting in the top seats

The request for the seats beside Jesus in his glory could hardly have come at a more incongruous moment. He has just spoken not of glory but of humiliation, rejection and death. Perhaps they have picked up the words about rising again and are beginning to see that there may be some 'glory' beyond that death. Or, perhaps more likely, they may have simply fastened on the title 'the Son of man' with its associations of glory in the Old Testament, and filtered out the less welcome parts of what Jesus has said about how the mission of the Son of man is to be achieved. For whatever reason, they do seem to have put their foot in it rather seriously, and Jesus is not slow to point out to them the unwelcome implications of their request.

## Death and glory

The glory is to be real enough, but the way to it is through suffering, which Jesus refers to as a cup to be drunk and a baptism to be endured. If they want to share the glory, they must share the suffering too. Jesus' question in verse 38 sounds like a rhetorical question, and it is a surprise to find that it is answered at all, let alone that it is answered positively. The glib assurance of their reply 'We are able' is breathtaking, but perhaps it betrays not so much a conscious claim to be ready and able to share all that Jesus will undergo as a still inadequate grasp of what he has been talking about.

One day they will indeed suffer in their turn, James as one of the first Christian martyrs (Acts 12:2) and John, according to tradition, as a prisoner on the isle of Patmos. But that suffering will not in itself earn them the places of honour which they covet. 'Promotion' in the kingdom of God is not won by aggressive self-presentation or even by martyrdom. It is for God, not us, to determine how its 'honours' are distributed. In the light of this chapter so far, we may be sure that it will not be on the sort of basis that human society takes for granted. It will be the little ones who will be the greatest in the kingdom of God.

## FOR MEDITATION

*It is easy to pour scorn on the crass self-assertion of James and John. But how far have we, after two thousand years to absorb the values of the kingdom of God, yet managed to escape from the world's concepts of status and importance?*

# 70

## MARK 10:41-45
## 'Not so among you'

At first sight you might imagine that the indignation of the other ten against James and John sprang from a holy disapproval of their failure to grasp the principles of the kingdom of God. But a much less flattering explanation suggests itself when we note that Jesus' stern words in verses 42–44 are addressed not to James and John, but to the other ten, who apparently deserve a rebuke no less than the two brothers. Their anger, then, probably arose from the much more unspiritual cause of their annoyance that the other two had got in first, and tried to steal a march on them by claiming the top seats in advance!

## Rulers and great ones

By now we are familiar with Jesus' reversal of the world's ideas of greatness and leadership. But this is the most powerful statement yet of the contrast between the way society operates and the way it is in the kingdom of God. It is specifically 'the Gentiles' whom Jesus singles out for comparison, but the desire to impose your authority on everyone else is not an exclusively Gentile trait! Perhaps he mentions them specifically because under Roman occupation the Jews had less opportunity to be 'lords' and 'tyrants', and resented the domineering attitude of their imperial overlords.

But all this is quite the opposite of the way the kingdom of God operates, where greatness is in service and the slave is master. 'It is not so among you' could be written as a motto over all this part of the Gospel. The disciples are learning, painfully, that this new movement into which they have come does not work like other human movements. It is an alternative society, in which the first are last and the last first. Wherever we see the stratifications and divisions which human society takes for granted we need to remind ourselves, 'not so among you'.

# The supreme model

It was the destiny of the 'Son of man' that 'all peoples, nations and languages should serve him' (Daniel 7:14). Yet Jesus, the Son of man in whom Daniel's prophecy is fulfilled, came not to be served but to serve. And in serving he would also fulfil another great prophecy of the Old Testament, the portrait of God's suffering Servant in Isaiah chapters 42 and 53, one who was to be God's chosen, anointed with his Spirit and sent to fulfil his mission of mercy and judgment, and yet who would accomplish this mission by suffering and death, dying for the sins of his people.

The words 'to give his life a ransom for many' echo the language of Isaiah 53:10–12. This is about as close as Jesus will get in Mark's Gospel to spelling out *why* his death is necessary, and what it is intended to achieve. The words are brief and allusive, but they point unmistakably to that great passage Isaiah 52:13—53:12 in which the Christian church has ever since seen a clear blueprint for what Jesus would achieve on the cross: 'He was wounded for our transgressions, crushed for our iniquities; upon him was the punishment that made us whole, and by his bruises we are healed; the Lord has laid on him the iniquity of us all.'

All this is a model for our imitation, not of course in his specific role of being a ransom for many—only he could do that, and it need never be done again—but in the utter neglect of self-interest which enabled him to choose death 'for many' rather than the glory which was his due.

## FOR MEDITATION

*Read again Isaiah 52:13—53:12, and think about what it meant for Jesus to fulfil that vision. And then reflect that in this he is a model for us!*

# 71

## MARK 10:46-52
# Another blind man

Act 2, which began with the healing of a blind man (8:22–26) now comes to its close with another. The treatment of the disciples' spiritual blindness which has been such a prominent feature of the intervening chapters will now give way to the rapidly unfolding events which follow on Jesus' arrival in Jerusalem. The time of preparation is over, and the last act is about to begin.

## Last stop before Jerusalem

Jericho, in the Jordan valley, is the last town to be passed by the pilgrim on the way to Jerusalem. The steep desert road will lead up from here into the hills where the capital stands. For the first time in Mark's story, Jesus is about to come to the city of David, the site of the great temple which has been for a thousand years the focus of Israel's relationship with their God. By now the disciple group has gathered a large crowd of fellow-travellers, all going up to Jerusalem for the Passover festival. They are impatient to be there, and have no desire to be detained by a mere blind beggar; they tell him, roughly, to be quiet.

## From darkness to light

But this man, like the children in 10:13, is one of the 'little ones', the people who matter in the kingdom of God. Despite the crowd, Jesus hears his shouts, and stops. And the whole cavalcade stops with him, such is Jesus' authority. Now, following Jesus' lead, they change from rough rejection to encouraging acceptance, and the man has his wish granted. He stands before Jesus.

The cure is told simply, in an almost matter-of-fact way. The theme is familiar: it is faith which is the key to healing, faith which in this case has been demonstrated by his persistence in drawing Jesus' attention despite the crowd's rebuff, and by his simple assumption that Jesus, the 'teacher', has the authority to restore his sight. It is interesting that he twice addresses Jesus as 'Son of David': it is as the

146

Messiah, Son of David, on his way to the city of David, that Jesus has the authority to heal. This title, here used by the blind man for the first time in Mark's Gospel, will be taken up with enthusiasm by the crowds when they get to Jerusalem (11:10).

## 'On the way'

If we were right in concluding that the two stories of the healing of blind men have a symbolic dimension, there is special significance in the way this story ends. That the man, now able to see and therefore to travel, wants to join Jesus on his journey to Jerusalem is not in itself very surprising, but Mark's addition of the phrase 'on the way' suggests more. We read in Acts (9:2; 19:9, 23; 24:14, 22) that the early Christian movement was sometimes known as 'The Way', and this seems to have been one of their favourite terms for themselves. Does Mark then use the term here to indicate that once our spiritual blindness is cured the next step is to set out, with Jesus and his disciples, on the 'way' of discipleship?

### PRAYER

*Lord, Son of David, give us the faith to know that you can meet our need, the persistence not to be put off, and the determination to follow you 'on the way'.*

# 72 The arrival of the king

## Passover time

It is important to remember that in the week or two leading up to Passover large numbers of pilgrims would be arriving in Jerusalem, which at this time of the year had to accommodate something like six times its normal population. Jesus and his disciples would not be the only pilgrims coming up the road from Jericho. This was the way most Galilean pilgrims would arrive. So the crowd who 'went ahead and followed' (v. 9) would be mainly from Galilee. The excited shouts of verses 9 and 10 are not those of the people of Jerusalem, but of northerners, like Jesus and his disciples, arriving for the festival. The verdict of the people of Jerusalem will be given later, and it will be very different: 'Crucify him!' (15:11–15).

## A deliberate messianic gesture

Act 3 begins with the long-heralded arrival of Jesus in the capital city, for the first (and last) time in Mark's story. And he does it in style. This is the only time Jesus is recorded as riding rather than walking. He has walked more than a hundred miles, and surely does not *need* a ride so close to his journey's end. But among so many pilgrims on foot a mounted person will be conspicuous. And those who know their prophetic scriptures will immediately recognize what he is enacting: 'Lo, your king comes to you [Jerusalem]; triumphant and victorious is he, humble and riding on a donkey' (Zechariah 9:9).

So far Jesus has not allowed his disciples to talk openly about him as the Messiah. Even now it is in act rather than in words that the claim is made, and it will not be until 14:61–62 that he will himself state his messianic identity in so many words. But the time has now come to begin to call people to decision.

The event has been carefully prepared. In a village a mere two miles from the gates of Jerusalem a donkey (presumably belonging to a local supporter of Jesus) is ready to be collected, and at the given password his disciples are allowed to take it for Jesus' use. The apparently spontaneous provision of a 'red carpet' of clothes and branches may well have been orchestrated by the disciples, for all these people have already been travelling together up the long road from Jericho (10:46). The arrival has been deliberately staged to make a point.

## The kingdom of David

The shouts of the pilgrim crowd show that they have not missed the point. They have understood the acted allusion to Zechariah 9:9. Jerusalem's king is coming into his capital, and he comes to re-establish the long-lost kingdom of David. It was David who first set up his capital in Jerusalem, and it was his descendants who had reigned there until the Babylonians destroyed it six hundred years earlier. Since then there had been no Davidic king on the throne in Jerusalem, but now the 'Son of David' (10:47, 48) is coming. The messianic hopes of all the prophets, that one day God would set up a new king like David to restore the fortunes of his people, are all coming to fruition.

So Jesus, the prophet from the north, throws down the gauntlet to the authorities of the capital city. Will they recognize in this popular but already suspect teacher from Galilee 'the one who comes in the name of the Lord'?

**FOR MEDITATION**

*'Hosanna' means 'Save us', though it had also come to be used as simply a shout of praise. What sort of 'salvation' do you think the crowds were looking for? How would their hopes relate to what Jesus had in fact come to do?*

# A demonstration in the temple

Mark has carefully interwoven two themes here, as the scene shifts repeatedly between the temple and a fig tree on the Bethany road, thus: Verse 11, temple; verses 12–14, fig tree; verses 15–19, temple; verses 20–25, fig tree; verse 27, temple (which will then be the setting until the end of chapter 12). We have noted before Mark's tendency to 'sandwich' stories in this way, and when he does so it is usually because he wants us to notice a connection between them. We shall consider what that connection is in the next study, and we shall leave the fig tree until then. For now, we must focus on the temple.

## The national sanctuary

There were many synagogues but only one temple. Since Solomon's time this had been the focus of national religion, and more, a symbol of Israel's national identity. Surrounding the sanctuary itself was a vast complex of buildings and courtyards covering some 30 acres. The buildings were massive and magnificent ('He who has not seen Herod's temple has not seen a beautiful building', said the rabbis), and were the focus of intense national pride and patriotism. Anyone who treated the temple with disrespect could expect to be fiercely opposed, and might well be killed.

Jesus first of all visited the temple, as any visitor to the city would (v. 11). He 'looked around at everything' but did nothing on this first day. This was probably more than simply sight-seeing. When Jesus comes back next day he will be ready to take decisive action, and this first visit may well have been the opportunity for planning his next move, or, as the crime-writers would say, 'casing the joint'.

## Holy violence

The stalls of the traders were set up before the Passover in the 'Court of the Gentiles', the huge open area surrounding the inner courts and the sanctuary itself. This was a place of general concourse, not a worship area as such, though it was the closest that a non-Jewish visitor was allowed to get to the sanctuary. The stalls were set up with the approval of the temple authorities and fulfilled the useful, indeed necessary, purpose of enabling visitors to change their money into the special coinage needed for temple offerings, and to buy the animals needed for sacrifice. But to Jesus they were a symbol of debased worship and a distraction from the prayer which all nations should be able to offer in God's house.

He apparently cleared them out single-handed, such was his personal authority (together with the element of surprise?). It was a gesture which not surprisingly excited the implacable hostility of the temple authorities. So why did he do it?

It was more than a spontaneous expression of his disgust at the misuse of a holy place. Like the entry to Jerusalem the previous day, it was a defiant gesture, embodying a messianic claim. Those who saw it might have thought of Malachi 3:1–4, which speaks of the Lord suddenly coming in judgment to his temple and purifying the descendants of Levi. Or they might remember the prophecy that in the day when God restores his people 'there shall no longer be traders in the house of the Lord' (Zechariah 14:21). The restoration of the temple was one of the tasks the Messiah was expected to perform, and here was Jesus setting about it with a will. He left the temple authorities with little choice: if they did not accept his claim, they must oppose such a flagrant attack on their authority to the death.

## FOR MEDITATION

*Is what Jesus did in the temple an encouragement for his followers to use violence? If so, when and for what reasons? If not, what is the difference?*

# 74 The fruitless fig tree

## A pointless display of power?

Interwoven with Jesus' attack on the traders in the temple is the story of his cursing and destruction of a fig tree because it had no fruit. Jesus' other miracles save life and restore health, but this one seems quite out of character. It is apparently wantonly destructive and serves no useful purpose.

But by linking it with the story of Jesus' demonstration in the temple Mark suggests that, even if in itself it achieved no good, its value is to be seen rather in what the fate of the fig tree symbolizes. The temple has proved to be equally barren and disappointing, and can expect a similar fate. In chapter 13 Jesus will take up the theme of the temple's destruction more fully.

## Leaves and fruit

So how does the fig tree represent the temple? It was all leaves and no fruit, show without substance, promise without performance. The disappointment of the hungry traveller on reaching a promising tree and finding it empty represents God's disappointment with his people's worship. (See Micah 7:1; Jeremiah 8:13 for exactly the same imagery.) What happened to the fig tree is what may also be expected to happen to the temple whose outward show hides an empty performance.

Mark does rather complicate matters, however, by his comment that in any case 'it was not the season for figs'—so how could the poor tree be blamed for not having any? Figs are not harvested until June, but at Passover season in Jerusalem the fig trees have begun to come into leaf, and at that time there are early green figs already on the trees. They are not very palatable so early in the year, but can be eaten if there is nothing else (I have tried them!). But this tree, for all its show of leaves, did not even have any of these early figs to offer.

# Have faith in God

By his placing of the story, then, Mark has suggested its symbolic dimension. But the lesson which is explicitly drawn out from it is not about the temple, but about the sheer power which Jesus has shown in the complete withering up of the tree in a mere twenty-four hours. It is this, rather than any underlying symbolism, which has aroused Peter's amazement, and the suggestion is that such an act of power must be unique.

Not at all, says Jesus. You can do even more amazing things if you have faith in God. Throwing a mountain into the sea is not on the face of it any more useful a miracle than destroying a fig tree, but it is undeniably spectacular; it represents what is from a human perspective impossible. But it is not impossible for God. So it all depends on faith, which is the secret to experiencing the power of God in answer to prayer.

Verses 22–24 have an unqualified sound which many rightly find uncomfortable. Does Jesus really mean that we can have just whatever we like, so long as we believe it? Why then have so many 'believing' prayers remained unanswered? But this is to treat faith as a magical formula, rather than what it really is, a relationship of trust in a heavenly Father. If that relationship is real, there will be no room for selfish or inappropriate prayers.

## PRAYER

*Lord, give us the faith which can ask and receive according to your will—and so may you not find us unfruitful.*

# 75

# The challenge from officialdom

Jesus is back in the Court of the Gentiles, the ideal place for gathering a crowd for teaching, but a place on which he has already stamped his authority in a different way when he drove out the traders. After so public a challenge to the powers that be he can hardly have expected to return there without facing official sanctions, and now he is confronted by a very high-level delegation: the chief priests, scribes and elders were the three groups who made up the Sanhedrin, the supreme Jewish religious council. It was their responsibility to maintain orthodoxy in matters of religion, and Jesus is very definitely under investigation.

## By what authority?

'These things' must refer primarily to what Jesus has just done in the temple courtyard. This, and his dramatic entry to the city, are his only public actions yet recorded in Jerusalem, and the two symbolic acts together do in fact add up to what looks like a quite outrageous claim—unless it is true. Anyone who throws his weight about in this way must expect to be called to account. What right has he to assume such a high-profile role, and one which by implication is a challenge to the existing authorities? So their question is a fair one: who has given him authority to behave like this?

Jesus' reply looks like a clever cop-out. He hinges his reply to their question on their first replying to his, and makes sure that the question he asks them is one they will not want to answer. They know very well what they think about John the Baptist, of course: he was a charlatan who got what he deserved. But they dare not say so publicly, because that is not how ordinary Jews felt about John. So Jesus is let off the hook, and the encounter ends in a stalemate.

# John and Jesus

But while Jesus has indeed cleverly got out of a tight corner, his reply was not merely a clever debating ploy. By bringing John the Baptist into the discussion he has in fact made, by implication, a very important claim. For the logic of his reply is that whatever conclusion they come to about John's authority must also apply to his own. So just as other people have interpreted Jesus as a second John the Baptist (6:14; 8:28), Jesus himself now endorses that view. If John came with authority 'from heaven', Jesus' authority is no less. And the way people have responded to John's preaching is likely to determine the way they respond to Jesus as well. As in 9:12–13 Jesus linked John's fate with his own, so now he also links himself to John's heaven-sent authority.

So Jesus' answer to the officials' question is clear: his authority, like John's, is 'from heaven'. But he will not give them the satisfaction of hearing him say so in so many words, for any such explicit claim would be sure to be used against him (as indeed it will be when eventually he declares himself openly to the Sanhedrin in 14:61–64).

## PRAYER

*Lord, may our prejudices not keep us from recognizing*
*your authority and gladly living under it, even when it means*
*accepting that we may have been wrong.*

# 76 Getting rid of the son

In the last study we heard Jesus' claim, by implication, to divine authority for what he was doing. Now the same claim is made, this time in the form of a fictional story with a transparent meaning. His opponents know exactly what he means (v. 12), but they can do nothing about it yet.

## The tenants of the vineyard

The tenants were under contract to supply a fixed proportion of each year's produce to the absentee landowner, but rent collectors were no more popular then than now. Of course there is an element of exaggeration, even of burlesque, in the violence with which the tenants treated the messengers, and still more in their naive assumption that if they killed the son and heir they would somehow gain a right to the property. But this is not a depiction of real life, but a story meant to convey a message.

## What the story means

A Jewish audience, hearing a story about a vineyard which failed, would surely think of Isaiah's famous allegory of Israel as God's vineyard, which disappointed him by producing only 'wild grapes' (Isaiah 5:1-7). So the vineyard is Israel, and the owner is God. When the Jerusalem authorities 'realized that he had told this parable against them' (v. 12), they recognized the allegory and saw themselves and their predecessors in the role of the defaulting tenants. The servants, then, are the prophets, who often enough in the Old Testament suffered rejection and even death for faithfully calling God's people back to their true allegiance.

So who is the son, whose death is the climax of the story and will provoke the landowner to take decisive action against the tenants? Jesus does not say, but then he surely does not need to. This is as near as he will get to making a public claim to be the Son of God until his ringing declaration before the Sanhedrin in 14:62. He comes to them, then, with the authority of his Father (as he has just implied in 11:27–33), and presents them with one last chance to respond to God's call. By killing him, they will be sealing their own fate, and the vineyard will be given to 'others'.

## The rejected stone

Jesus leaves it at that, and does not offer any interpretation of the story (though one is given in Matthew 21:43). Instead he adds a quotation from Psalm 118:22, about the rejected stone. What is rejected by human valuation may prove to be the very thing which God has chosen. The rejected stone becomes the cornerstone; the rejected Son will be the Lord of all. The message is clear enough. In setting themselves against Jesus they are taking the opposite side to God, and in the end those who oppose God cannot win. Jesus has no illusions about his coming death, but he can also see beyond it, to when 'the Lord's doing' will overturn all human attempts to hijack the kingdom of God.

**FOR MEDITATION**

*In what ways may we be in danger of setting ourselves against God's purpose and refusing him the produce which is his due? Has this parable any warning for us?*

# The poll tax

## A loaded question

When the Romans deposed Archelaus, the son of Herod, from his kingship in Judea and imposed direct rule from Rome, one of the most resented by-products was the imposition of a poll tax on all adult Jewish males, to be paid to the Roman state. Some patriots could not accept that the people of God should pay tax to a pagan king, and a serious armed revolt against the poll tax took place in AD6. That was not many years ago, and the poll tax still rankled; it was one of the main targets of the later Zealot revolt, and already a strong nationalist movement was growing again.

Jesus, as a Galilean, was not subject to this Judean tax. But to ask him, as a respected visiting teacher, to comment on it was a clever move. If he approved the tax he would immediately lose much popular support; if he opposed it he could be denounced to the Romans as a trouble-maker. So they had good grounds for hoping that they could 'trap him in what he said'.

## The significance of the coin

Jesus' first move is to ask them to show him a denarius, the Roman coin which was used for paying the poll tax. This apparently unnecessary request is in fact a clever way of discrediting his questioners. The silver denarius carried on it a portrait of the emperor and an inscription in which he was described as 'Son of God'. Both the 'graven image' and the wording were offensive to Jews, and the Romans, recognizing this, had sensibly arranged for copper coins to be minted for everyday use in Palestine which had no such portrait. Yet those who have come to Jesus with this political question can produce a denarius on the spot. If they are carrying the emperor's (idolatrous) coinage about with them, then they can have no grounds for refusing to pay his taxes!

# God and the emperor

But to show up the hypocrisy of his questioners is not in itself to answer the question, and it is an important one (and one which, in principle, applies to many other situations where a conflict of loyalties may arise between human government and our duty to God). So Jesus goes on to make his memorable pronouncement (more familiar in its traditional version, 'Render to Caesar...') which balances the duty to the emperor with the duty to God.

His words are enigmatic enough to allow him to escape the 'trap'. He throws back to the questioners the obligation to think out what are the limits of loyalty to God and to the state, and depending on your answer to that you might see Jesus as either opposing or supporting the payment of poll tax. But the important thing about Jesus' reply is that it assumes that there is room for *both* loyalties at the same time. According to the Zealot ideology loyalty to God ruled out submission to the Roman state, and obedience to Rome was rebellion against God. But for Jesus there is room for both.

Of course it is true that in the real world there will sometimes be a conflict between our religious and our political duty, as many Christians under despotic régimes know to their cost. Jesus gives us no clue here as to how such a conflict may be resolved. But what he does offer is the important principle that such conflict is the exception rather than the rule, and that in normal circumstances it is possible to be both a faithful disciple and a loyal citizen.

## PRAYER

*Lord, make us equally eager to serve you and to play our part as citizens of the society in which you have set us, and where the two seem to come into conflict, help us to see clearly what are 'the things that are God's'.*

# The God of the living

The Pharisees have failed to 'trap' Jesus. So now it is time for the Sadducees to try. They were a separate party within the Jewish hierarchy, and at many points were in opposition to the Pharisees, but they seem to be at one with them on the need to silence this radical new teacher. While the Pharisees believed in life after death, the Sadducees rejected this as a new and unfounded teaching, and so now they test Jesus to find out how he will line up on this controversial issue.

## Another trick question

So they set Jesus up with a trick question. It depends on the Old Testament regulation (Deuteronomy 25:5–6) which provided for the wife of a man who died childless to become the wife of his brother and so to 'raise up children for his brother'—and thus to provide him the only form of immortality the Sadducees would recognize. This legislation was still in force, at least in theory, at the time of Jesus, and so it was theoretically possible for the same woman to be the wife of seven brothers, though their story is more likely a fictional case designed to pour scorn on the idea of an after-life. But of course the issue is a real one for anyone who believes in life after death, since many people are in fact married more than once, whether because of death or divorce, and in such cases the idea of reunion after death can pose a problem.

## 'Like angels in heaven'

There are two levels to the question, first that of married relations after death, and second the more fundamental issue of whether there is life after death at all. Jesus deals with both levels in turn.

But first he exposes the basis of their scepticism: they are ignorant both of scripture and of the power of God. Their outlook is limited to human logic and human possibilities, and so cannot cope with the concept of life after death which necessarily falls outside their current experience. In this they are typical of the secular thinking which we know so well today, which has no room for anything beyond our immediate experience.

So the answer to the first level of the question is that we must not picture life in heaven as being just the same as life on earth. Where there is no death there is no need for procreation, and so the exclusive relationship within which procreation takes place is no longer appropriate: 'they neither marry nor are given in marriage'. This is not to say that there is no love, but there is no need for the exclusiveness and jealousy which are an essential part of married life on earth. We may hope that Jesus speaks not of something lost, but of something gained in heaven.

## Why there must be life after death

The underlying issue of what happens when we die is dealt with in a very compressed argument in verses 26–27. It depends on the character of God, and of the relationship into which he enters with those who are privileged to be his people. When God identified himself to Moses as the God of Abraham, Isaac and Jacob (Exodus 3:6), those three worthies had already been dead for several centuries. Could God, the living God, enter into a solemn covenant with Abraham and his descendants only to see it end in death? Could he describe himself as the God of someone who was now nothing more than a memory? God's covenant cannot be so easily broken, nor his 'steadfast love' so temporary. It is an obscurely brief argument, but behind it lies a satisfying theology of life and not death, and of the faithfulness of God, which makes no sense without a resurrection to eternal life.

### PRAYER

*Lord, give us the boldness to reach beyond the limitations of our human experience, and to believe even where we cannot yet see.*

# 79

# The two great commandments

This is another tricky question, since an unwise answer could expose Jesus to the charge of not valuing some other aspect of the Old Testament law. To find a commandment in the Old Testament which really does sum up all the rest calls for great wisdom. But the atmosphere this time is not so hostile as before, and the questioner, who is already aware that Jesus is worth listening to (v. 28), is quite prepared to concede that he has given a good answer.

## God and my neighbour

The first commandment selected by Jesus would come as no surprise. Deuteronomy 6:4–5 had already been singled out as the basic requirement of the law, and was recited daily by all pious Jews. What is creative about Jesus' reply is that he links with it a less prominent commandment from Leviticus 19:18, 'You shall love your neighbour as yourself'. And the result is to cover the full scope of the law, which is concerned not only with our duty to God but with how we treat other people. The first four of the ten commandments deal with our duty to God, and the other six with our duty to our neighbour. When you think about it, there is not much in the Old Testament law which does not come under one or other of these headings.

And the key word in both texts is 'love'. Love goes behind the outward acts which the law commands to include also the attitude and motive for doing them. This will become a key theme of Christian teaching as it develops in the New Testament: 'love is the fulfilling of the law' (Romans 13:8–10; 1 Corinthians 13, etc.).

## 'Not far from the kingdom of God'

The scribe immediately catches the point. He admires the comprehensiveness of Jesus' answer, but he also recognizes the new perspective which it offers. In practice what concerned the scribes from day to day was mainly the practical implementation of the law, particularly its ritual requirements, the 'whole burnt offerings and sacrifices'. It was easy for this to get so much out of proportion that the underlying purpose was forgotten, and the 'love' element became a casualty. Jesus has redressed the balance, and the scribe can immediately see the liberating force of this new summary of the law. It is putting first things first, and putting the 'burnt offerings and sacrifices' in their place.

Such a clear sense of priorities shows that the scribe and Jesus are fighting on the same side. For the kingdom of God is about love rather than burnt offerings and sacrifices. Once the man has recognized that, he is not far from the kingdom of God. We do not know whether he became a disciple, but surely his attitude to his scribal duties could never be the same again.

There can be no answer to such a far-reaching pronouncement which was so obviously 'right'. Jesus' teaching is in a different league from normal scribal debate. No wonder that from now on 'no one dared ask him any question'!

## FOR MEDITATION

*How wide-ranging are the implications of Jesus' summary of the law? How can we love God with all our heart, soul, mind and strength? And what does it mean to love our neighbours as ourselves? How far have my attitudes and actions today matched up to these commandments?*

# 80

# David's Lord

Now that all his questioners have been silenced, it is time for Jesus to take the initiative and in his turn to pose a tricky question. But instead of putting his opponents on the spot, he goes straight on to answer his own question. Or rather he answers it with another question, which is then left hanging in the air. We readers, like the crowds in the Jerusalem temple, are left to work out for ourselves what his rhetorical question implies.

The issue is, on the face of it, a purely 'academic' discussion about what is the right terminology to describe the Messiah. But in view of the increasingly strong hints we have seen in Mark's story, we may be sure that many of Jesus' hearers understood that it was not Messiahship in the abstract that he was talking about, but his own mission. He may not yet have openly called himself the Messiah, but his actions and teaching have left little doubt that he saw himself in that light.

## The Son of David

The blind man at Jericho appealed to Jesus as 'Son of David', and the pilgrim crowds escorting Jesus into Jerusalem were expecting him to bring in 'the coming kingdom of our ancestor David'. Jews at that time had a variety of ideas about the 'Messiah', the one whom God was going to send as his agent in the last days. But one element which almost all of them would have had in common would be the hope that in some sense the kingdom of David would be restored. 'Son of David' was a title calculated to arouse messianic excitement.

It was also a title which early Christians had no hesitation in applying to Jesus. Matthew in particular emphasizes and defends Jesus' role as Son of David, and Paul takes it for granted as basic to the Christian gospel (Romans 1:3). Yet here is Jesus questioning the title and apparently repudiating it. So what is going on?

# More than a son

Jesus' argument, drawn from Psalm 110:1, is about status. If, as both Jesus and his audience would naturally assume, the psalm was written by the great David himself, then there is someone whom even that supreme king referred to as his 'Lord'. Yet that person cannot be God, since in the psalm he is addressed *by* God. That person must then be the Messiah, still to come in the future to bring to completion the work which David has begun. (This too would be common ground: the psalm was understood to be about the future Messiah.)

In that case the Messiah is not merely another David, still less someone who, as his son, is under his authority. Rather he is David's 'Lord', or, as the hymn-writer puts it 'Great David's *greater* Son'. So the trouble with the title 'Son of David' is not that it claims too much. but that it claims too little.

# The wrong vibes

Another problem with the title 'Son of David' was that for most Jews it would carry an inevitably nationalistic and political overtone. David was a great warrior, whose victories established the greatest empire Israel ever possessed. Now Israel was again under foreign rule as it had been under the Philistines before David took over. So a 'Son of David' must have as his primary task the restoration of Israel's fortunes, and that could only mean armed rebellion against Rome. Is it any wonder then that Jesus found it necessary to question the title? It would, in the wrong hands, commit him to a mission very different from what he had come to do.

So, as usual, Jesus is in the business of asking people to reconsider their fundamental assumptions, and not to limit him and his mission to what they have been expecting and hoping for.

**PRAYER**

*Lord, help us to realize that your agenda may not be the same as ours, and to be prepared to accept your Lordship on your terms, not ours.*

# 81 A telling contrast

In these verses a scathing attack on the hypocrisy of the religious professionals is followed by an example of true piety. But the example is not of a prominent religious figure, but of a poor widow whom everyone (and especially the scribes?) would overlook. Truly, the first shall be last and the last first.

## The first shall be last (verses 38–40)

Not all scribes were as bad as this, of course, as we have just seen in verses 28–34. But the pattern of outward show combined with inner corruption is an occupational hazard of religious professionals, now as much as then. 'Let anyone who is without sin cast the first stone.'

We all like to be noticed, and to be respected by others. But there are some who go out of their way to achieve this, just as the 'great ones' among the Gentiles lord it over others (10:42). And when it is those in a position of religious leadership who do this, it is particularly inappropriate. But it is still worse when their real behaviour does not match their pretensions, when they prey on the vulnerable, and cover up their greed by a show of piety. Such hypocrisy on the part of 'religious' people rightly draws the scorn of those who are able to see through the pretence. The words are strong, but the scenario is not imaginary. The history of the Christian church offers us conspicuous examples of such hollow profession, and no doubt there have been, as there are now, plenty of less prominent but no less pathetic examples.

## The last shall be first (verses 41–44)

It is a relief to turn to someone quite the opposite, someone who had no desire to be noticed, and who would have been as surprised as Jesus' disciples must have been if she had heard what Jesus said to them about her. She was a person of no importance, and she knew it. But she loved God, and gave the little she had to him.

Contributing to the temple funds was a very public business. A row of thirteen large collecting boxes were lined up in the Court of the Women (the point in the temple beyond which only men could go), and people could and did go there to watch. And no doubt many of those who put money into the boxes were not at all reluctant to be seen, and made sure that the size of their donation was clearly visible.

Jesus' comment to his disciples is typical of what he has been teaching them on the way to Jerusalem about the values of the kingdom of God. The natural human perspective is to welcome and make much of the big donor, and to treat the poor widow with at best a condescending greeting. But in the kingdom of God her total dedication counts for far more than an easily spared fortune.

## FOR MEDITATION

*In my church, and among my own personal acquaintance, who are the people I most respect and admire? Are they the ones Jesus would put first?*

*What can we do to develop the values of the kingdom of God within our own congregations?*

# 82

# The temple to be destroyed

The temple has been the scene of most of Jesus' activity and teaching since he arrived in Jerusalem. Now he leaves it, never to return, and as he leaves he utters words which must have shocked his disciples profoundly. No wonder that yet again some of them will have to ask him to explain privately what he means (vv. 3–4).

## Herod's Temple

The original temple, built by Solomon, was destroyed by the Babylonians in the sixth century. Its replacement, built towards the end of the sixth century, survived until the time of Herod the Great, who began the process of replacing the old structure with a magnificent complex of buildings worthy of the nation's capital. By the time of Jesus' public ministry the replacement was still not complete, but already it was one of the architectural wonders of the world. The huge, finely dressed stones which make up the lower part of the 'Western Wall' in Jerusalem today give only a hint of the magnificence of the temple itself; they are only a part of the substructure, the huge artificial platform on which the temple proper stood. Of the temple buildings themselves not a trace survives (as Jesus predicted).

## Not one stone upon another

Jesus' Galilean disciples are, understandably, awestruck by what they see. There is nothing to match this in their Galilean towns and villages. But Jesus is impressed not by the appearance of the temple, but by what he knows will soon be its fate. The 'house of God' is to be utterly destroyed. A generation later, when the Romans conquered Jerusalem in AD70, his prediction would be literally fulfilled.

Jesus was not the first to utter such an oracle against the temple. Micah in the eighth century (Micah 3:12) and Jeremiah in the sixth (Jeremiah 26) had said the same—and then too it had proved true when the Babylonians came. But such an unpopular and 'unpatriotic' message had nearly cost Jeremiah his life, and Jesus' words are not likely to have been any more popular. If there was one thing on which almost all Jews could agree, it was the importance and the sanctity of the temple. It was God's house, and its destruction was unthinkable. Anyone who spoke against it was speaking against God and against Israel. As we shall see later, Jesus' words against the temple stuck in people's minds, and were ready to be used against him (14:58; 15:29). Whatever you thought of the rest of his teaching and actions, an attack on the temple was unforgivable.

## A symbol of a new order

But this was not the first time Jesus had provoked such anger. When he drove the traders out of the Court of the Gentiles (11:15–18) it was an expression of his repudiation of what the temple had become, and Mark, by interweaving that story with the cursing of the fruitless fig tree, has heightened the sense of doom. This temple, with all its magnificent stones, was merely a 'temple made with hands', and what God was now preparing through the ministry of Jesus was a new temple 'not made with hands' (14:58). The old order, focused on a single nation and its national shrine in the capital city, was soon to give way to a new order in which all nations would indeed find their house of prayer (11:17), not in a single building but in a faith community which would transcend all racial and political boundaries.

The disciples would understand very little of this at the time, but Jesus has sown a seed which will one day lead to a radically new understanding of what it means to be the people of God, in which there will be no place for this old temple made with hands.

### PRAYER

*Lord, may we be impressed not by outward show and magnificence, but by holiness and truth. Teach us not to cling to the wrong things, but to be open to new ways as we follow you.*

# 83 The disciples' question

It may seem out of proportion to devote a whole study to one question. But the interpretation of the chapter which follows is controversial, and the question to which the following discourse (vv. 5–37) provides the answer is an important key to understanding it. So to think first about the opening question gives us the opportunity also to gain an overview of the discourse as a whole.

## An interlude in the drama

We have seen that in the middle of Act 1 Mark has placed a lengthy section of teaching (4:1–34) to give the reader the opportunity to think about the implications of the story which has been unfolding so rapidly up to that point. Now in the middle of Act 3 we have a similar 'pause for breath'. From 11:1 onwards the confrontation between Jesus and the Jerusalem authorities has been building up to a climax, and in chapter 14 we shall witness the inevitable result in the arrest and trial of Jesus. But first in chapter 13 we can sit quietly with Jesus and the original four disciples on the Mount of Olives, looking across the Kidron valley to the temple buildings, and listen to Jesus speaking about what is soon to come.

It is in the temple that Jesus has acted and taught in such a way that he has antagonized the authorities, and his alleged attack on the temple will be a central element in his trial and condemnation. So it is appropriate that it is the future fate of the temple, with all that that implies, which is the starting point for this vision of what is to come. But interpreters do not agree on how far the rest of the chapter remains focused on the coming destruction of the temple, and how far it moves off into a more distant future.

## What are 'these things'?

The question in verse 4 picks up directly from Jesus' startling pronouncement in verse 2. They want to know when the temple will be destroyed, and how they may know when that time is coming. The question therefore does not suggest that there is anything more on the agenda than the event Jesus has predicted in verse 2.

The problem is that some of the language in the later part of the chapter speaks of what seems to be a more ultimate crisis, when the sun and moon are darkened and the Son of man is seen coming in clouds. And when Matthew relates the same discourse in chapters 24–25 of his Gospel, it is considerably expanded to include explicit language about the 'coming' (*parousia*, a technical term not used in Mark) of the Son of man and about the final judgment, while the disciples' question in Matthew asks not only about the destruction of the temple but also about 'the sign of your coming and of the end of the age'. There is no such language here in Mark, but is it possible that Mark understood 'all these things' to include more than just the events associated with the destruction of the temple?

## A minority view

This is where interpreters take different positions. Some think that chapter 13 is *all* about the destruction of the temple, while some think that much of it (and particularly verses 24–27) is about the second coming of Jesus. The author of these notes holds a view between these two positions: I believe that the bulk of the discourse, including verses 24–27, is a direct answer to the disciples' question, and refers to the destruction of the temple, which will happen within 'this generation' (v. 30), but that from verse 32 onwards a new note is introduced by speaking of a different 'day and hour', the time of Jesus' return to earth at some indefinite time in the future.

Since many would not agree with my interpretation, I thought it right to draw attention to its minority status at this point. I cannot argue the case here, but I trust that the notes which follow will help to explain why I understand the chapter in this way.

### FOR MEDITATION

*Try to imagine how you, as a first-century Galilean fisherman, would have reacted to what Jesus said in verse 2. What questions would be uppermost in your mind? What would you think would be the implications of the loss of the temple? What sort of assurances, and warnings, would you need from Jesus?*

# 84

# The beginning
# of the birth-pangs

The theme which runs through these verses is 'not yet'. They have asked for a 'sign' of the coming events, and Jesus replies by talking about things which are *not* as yet signs of the destruction of the temple. These are all necessary preliminaries, but 'the end is still to come'. This note of warning against getting excited too soon is in sharp contrast to the wording of verse 14, 'But when you see...'. *That* will be the time to take action, but all the events described in verses 5–13, however dramatic they may seem, are no more than preliminary skirmishes.

## Impostors

When Jesus himself is gone, the disciples will need to be on their guard against impostors. History confirms this need, as the Christian church has been visited by a long succession of people claiming to represent Jesus and trying, often by proclaiming the imminent end of the world, to gain influence over gullible believers. The warning will be repeated in verses 21–22, so the problem is clearly important. It is not very clear just how their claim 'I am' relates to the destruction of the temple. Perhaps they will claim that they have come to fulfil Jesus' prophecy, and to offer a new alternative to the doomed temple and its worship.

## Wars, earthquakes and famines

Another easy mistake will be to imagine that when catastrophic events happen in the world this is the sign that Jesus' prophecy is to be fulfilled. But there have been few ages of history which have not seen their share of 'wars and rumours of wars', of earthquakes and famines. Such news fills our newspapers still today. There were certainly plenty of wars, earthquakes and famines in the middle years of the first century, but when the disciples hear of them they are not to take them as signs of 'the end'. At most they are 'the beginning of the birth-pangs'—but who knows how long the labour will be?

## Opposition and persecution

Another recurrent feature of this interim period will be the experience of opposition and persecution. This too is not peculiar to the middle years of the first century. At many times during the first three centuries the Christian church faced the hostility of the Roman state. Ever since then Christians in various times and places have faced persecution, sometimes from the state, sometimes from local pressure groups, sometimes, it must be admitted, from other Christian groups and power structures.

The opposition Jesus describes is both Jewish ('councils' [literally Sanhedrins], 'synagogues') and Gentile ('governors and kings'). But it will not be a purely negative experience; rather it will provide the opportunity for 'testimony', and for the good news to be proclaimed to all nations. Mark has included in his Gospel increasing hints of the expansion of the 'Jesus movement' outside the bounds of Israel, and here is a clear indication that the good news is to reach all people, even if the means is through the Christian experience of persecution. The Holy Spirit, directing the disciples' words, will ensure that the opportunity is not lost.

The road of discipleship is not going to be easy, either in the days before the destruction of the temple or in the long centuries to follow when the experience of hostility will be ever present. But even when the whole world seems to be against them, they have the assurance that it is worth going on, for at the end of the road of endurance there is salvation for those whose suffering has been incurred 'because of me' (v. 9), 'because of my name' (v. 13). Those who follow Jesus on the way of the cross can expect no less.

**PRAYER**

*Lord, help us to endure. May we be less concerned with calculating 'the end' than with being faithful witnesses to the good news here and now, whatever it may cost.*

# 85
# Crisis in Judea

In AD70 the Romans captured Jerusalem and destroyed the temple and much of the city. That was the crucial turning point in the war of Jewish independence which began in AD66, even though resistance dragged on until the fall of Masada in AD73. Before Jerusalem fell, it endured a long and terrible siege, and it is that period which forms the background to Jesus' warnings in these verses.

## The desolating sacrilege

In 167BC the Syrian king Antiochus desecrated the temple in Jerusalem by setting up in it an idolatrous statue. It was that assault on the Jewish religion which sparked off the great Maccabean revolt. In the book of Daniel Antiochus' statue is referred to as 'the abomination which desolates' (Daniel 9:27; 11:31; 12:11). Jesus here predicts that in some way that dreadful event will be re-enacted, and when it is, that will be the time to take action, because his prediction of the destruction of the temple is about to be fulfilled. Just how it will be re-enacted the reader is left to 'understand' in the light of events, and it is not easy for us to be sure what Jesus had in mind. Perhaps he was thinking of the time just before the Roman siege began when the Zealot troops took over the sanctuary as a military headquarters, or perhaps of the bringing of the idolatrous Roman standards into the city when it was captured.

## The horrors of the siege

The Roman siege will be a time of unparalleled suffering (as indeed the graphic account by the contemporary Jewish historian Josephus makes clear), and those who have the opportunity to escape must use it urgently. It will be hard to get away in time, and those encumbered by young children or by pregnancy will be particularly vulnerable. If it occurs in winter, when weather conditions may be severe and the roads impassable, the suffering will be even greater. This is a portrayal of a national disaster of the first order.

But even in that time of disaster, God will not be absent. The fall of the city and the destruction of the temple, which might seem to be the triumph of a pagan power over the God of Israel, will take place only within the will of God, and the length and severity of that time of suffering remains under his control. For while the fate of Jerusalem is to be seen as God's judgment on a fruitless people, the city contains also those who are God's 'elect' (see also verse 27), his true people through whom his purpose for Israel is still to continue beyond the disaster. For their sake the suffering will be limited.

## A time of confusion

At such a time people search for answers, for some meaning in the chaos of events. And so it will be the perfect opportunity for those who wish to make an impression. 'False messiahs and false prophets' are usually waiting in the wings for such an opportunity, and they can be very plausible, especially when, as Jesus warns here, they can appeal to 'signs and omens' as proof of their bona fides. The signs (such as Jesus himself has refused to provide, 8:11–12) are presumably miraculous occurrences: we are warned often enough in the Bible that not all apparent miracles are indications that the person who performs them comes with God's authority. Still today even the elect, the true people of God, are too easily taken in by 'signs and wonders'. But for them it is not the spectacular claims and actions of these impostors which should count, but the words of Jesus: 'I have already told you everything'.

### PRAYER

*In times of confusion and of conflicting claims, give us the wisdom to perceive where your hand is at work, and to hold fast by your word.*

# 86

# The climax of judgment

So far Jesus has spoken of preliminary events, and of the siege of the city, but without specifically talking of the destruction of the temple—which is what the disciples had asked him about. The words 'But in those days, after that suffering...' seem to be about to bring us to that climax, but instead we read of heavenly portents and the Son of man coming in clouds. Most interpreters think that here Jesus has moved unaccountably to speak of the end of the world and of his own second coming, only to return awkwardly in verse 30 to events which will occur within 'this generation'. I beg to differ!

## Cosmic imagery for political events

The words of verses 24–25 are drawn from Isaiah 13:10 and 34:4, where the subject is not the end of the world but the fall of pagan powers, Babylon and Edom. This language was for Isaiah a vivid way of speaking of the political disruption of the familiar world-order, to be followed not by the end of everything, but by a new order; history will continue. Jesus' use of this language is therefore very appropriate for the fall of Jerusalem, the end of the old order under which the purpose of God has been focused on a single city. The change to a new structure of authority is effectively, if extravagantly, conveyed by the cosmic language of Old Testament prophecy.

## A new focus of authority

In place of the old régime comes a new ruler, the Son of man. We have seen earlier (8:38) that when Jesus used this title for himself he was drawing on the vision of Daniel 7:13–14, the vision of 'one like a son of man' who comes in clouds to the throne of God and is given dominion over all nations for ever. When Jerusalem loses its central place in the purpose of God, the Son of man will enter into his destined kingship, and will gather in his elect (see vv. 20 and 22) not merely from the people of Israel, but 'from the four winds'. Hitherto God's purpose has been focused on a national group, the 'chosen people' of Israel, with their capital in Jerusalem. Now, as Jerusalem loses its supremacy, an international people of God, the people of the Son of man, will be gathered. It is through the people of Jesus that God's purpose will then go forward.

## 'This generation will not pass'

Already Jesus has said that while some of his disciples are still alive they will see that the kingdom of God has come with power (9:1), and in 14:62 he will again speak, using the language of Daniel 7:13–14, of a mighty reversal which will be seen by those who have rejected him. The climax is fast approaching, and it will all happen within this generation. It will come as inevitably as summer follows spring. Just as the leaves on the fig tree are a sign, so Jesus' disciples will be able to recognize the events he has spoken of, and be ready for the dramatic change which is coming. Unlike other people in Jerusalem, they need not be taken by surprise, for what Jesus predicts will surely happen.

Thus, in highly coloured language drawn from the Old Testament, Jesus has answered the disciples' question, 'When will this [the destruction of the temple] be?'. It will be within the living generation. And by his choice of prophetic texts he has given them important clues for understanding the cataclysmic events which they and other Jews are soon to experience. What to others will seem to be the end will prove for the followers of Jesus to be a decisive new beginning, the reign of the Son of man.

### FOR MEDITATION

*If you had been a Jewish disciple of Jesus in the first century, what would have been the significance for you of the destruction of the temple? How would you have been able to relate it to Jesus' enthronement as the Son of man? And what has all this to say to a modern Gentile Christian?*

# 87 An unknown day

## A change of subject

So far Jesus has been talking in colourful language but with firm conviction of when a specific event, the destruction of the temple, will take place. His quite definite prediction that it will take place within 'this generation' is underscored with the assurance that they can trust his words, which 'will never pass away'. It is therefore surprising to read now of a day which Jesus does not claim to know, and which is known to no-one but God himself. Whereas he has spoken of signs which the disciples may observe as the fall of the temple comes near, he now speaks of a day which comes without warning, and for which they must be ready at any time. The change of atmosphere is startling. What 'day' or 'hour' is this that he now speaks of in such different terms?

Verse 32 sounds like a change of subject: 'But about *that*...'. No single 'day' or 'hour' has been mentioned so far in this chapter. Jesus has spoken of 'those days' (v. 24) and 'these things' (vv. 29, 30; see also verse 4), but what 'day' is this which, unlike 'these things', cannot be dated? It is at this point that I believe Jesus has moved from talking about the destruction of the temple (as a near and datable event) to the day of his own future return in judgment (at an unknown and unpredictable time). There is little enough in the words of this chapter to make the reference clear, but when we compare this little paragraph with the much longer parallel section in Matthew (24:36 onwards) and with language about the Second Coming in other parts of the New Testament, this seems the most likely interpretation.

## Reserved information

Jesus usually speaks with such authority and certainty that it is a shock to hear him say that there is something which he does not know. True, the order in which he lists those who do not know—people, angels, the Son—has the effect of placing him above the angels and next only to the Father. He is the highest authority next to God, but he is still ignorant on this one point, the time of his own triumphant return. This must be, from the point of view of Christian orthodoxy, a limitation imposed by his incarnation: while living a human life on earth he is subordinate to the Father in knowledge as well as in authority.

## Don't be caught out

If the Son does not know, then certainly we do not. Those who devote long hours to trying to puzzle out from the prophets a timetable for the end of the world are wasting their time. It is unknown, and it is meant to be unknown. So the only appropriate response is not calculation but constant readiness. The little parable of the slaves left in charge while their master is away makes the point simply and clearly. We must always be ready, so that we will not be found asleep on duty.

Just how we are to be ready is not spelled out. No-one can live on constant red alert. But while life consists mainly of the ordinary and the humdrum, and while the round of work and leisure, waking and sleeping, must go on, it is healthy for us to remember that wherever in that cycle we may be our stewardship should be always open to scrutiny. Responsibilities postponed may prove to have been left too long.

**PRAYER**

*Lord, help us to live day by day as citizens of heaven, alert to*
*your voice, and ready for your coming.*

# 88

# A woman to be remembered

It is now time to return from the interlude of teaching on the Mount of Olives, back to the doomed city. The lines of confrontation have been sharply drawn since Jesus arrived in chapter 11, and now the climax of the drama is fast approaching. Mark sets the scene with an elaborate 'sandwich'. In verses 1 and 12 he reminds us that the setting is the Passover festival; in verses 1–2 and 10–11 he introduces us to those who at this sacred time are plotting Jesus' death; but within this framework he has set a powerful little story (vv. 3–9) which gives us a further insight into how Jesus himself is preparing for what he knows is soon to happen. In this study we concentrate on the story of the anointing of Jesus. In the next we shall return to the priests and Judas.

## What a waste!

Bethany, a village just over the hill from Jerusalem, was where Jesus and his disciples had found lodgings for their visit to the crowded city (11:11–12). An unnamed woman (John tells us it was Mary, the sister of Martha and Lazarus) performs an extravagant act of devotion by anointing Jesus' head with extremely expensive ointment. A single flask of ointment which could have been sold for nearly a year's wages must surely have been a family heirloom. To break open the jar and pour the whole lot over the head of this visitor was incredibly wasteful, and people are not slow to protest. There were so many more productive ways in which such a valuable possession could have been used. This is sheer irresponsibility.

## A matter of priorities

Jesus has often spoken in favour of the poor, and indeed has demanded of a rich man that he sell all his possessions and give the proceeds to the poor. So why does he not join in condemning this woman's squandering of such a valuable resource? It is a matter of priorities. To help the poor is good, but on this particular occasion to 'waste' the ointment on Jesus is better, for it is a unique opportunity. Her extravagant gift is a symbolic act of deep significance, and an example to be remembered. There is room in the kingdom of God both for the careful stewardship of resources for the sake of those in need, and, on occasion, for spontaneous and uncalculating devotion. True discipleship embraces not only scrupulous accountancy but also reckless exuberance. There is 'a time to gather… and a time to throw away' (Ecclesiastes 3:5–6).

## Death and good news

So what is so special about anointing Jesus with expensive ointment? It is 'a good service', not only because it beautifully expresses her devotion but also because, whether she knows it or not, she is pouring the ointment on what will in a few days be a hastily buried corpse, lacking the proper treatment with aromatic spices (see 16:1). Her act thus brings Jesus' death firmly into the picture, and Jesus himself welcomes its symbolism. He has come to Jerusalem to die, and his disciples must not be allowed to forget it. But that death is foreshadowed not in bleak horror and despair, but in the rich smell of a sumptuous ointment. There is something almost bizarre in speaking about burial and 'good news' in the same breath, but that is how Jesus' death will be. It will be proclaimed with joy in the whole world, and when it is, this woman's spontaneous act will be part of the story. What a wonderful way to be remembered!

### FOR MEDITATION
*In what ways may it be right for us to be extravagant in our service to Christ? Would you have joined the scolding in verse 5?*

# The priests and Judas Iscariot

## The plot against Jesus

We have had plenty of indications of how the religious authorities are reacting to Jesus. Even as far back as 3:6 they were plotting his death. Now he is in Jerusalem, within their grasp, and the time has come. But the same Passover festival which has brought Jesus to Jerusalem has also brought thousands of other pilgrims to the temple, and many of them already know Jesus, and are his enthusiastic supporters—as the pilgrim crowds have demonstrated when they escorted him into the city with shouts of Hosanna. To make an open move against Jesus would be likely to provoke a riot.

During the day, Jesus spent his time in the temple, very publicly. The only answer, then, is to try to arrest him at night, when there are no crowds of supporters around. But how do you find one among 100,000 Passover visitors? The city was far too small for the crowds who came at festival time, and the visitors spread out to the surrounding villages or camped on the hillsides around the city. They must find inside information of where Jesus and his disciples are staying.

## The informer

And that is where Judas comes in. His betrayal of Jesus consists firstly in his willingness to tell the authorities where the disciple group may be found at night, and indeed, as we shall see, to lead them there in person and identify Jesus so that they can arrest him. This is the service they most need from him, and it is for this that he is to be well paid. We shall see also, however, that when Jesus is brought to trial the high priest will be well informed about the sort of things Jesus has been saying about himself and his mission. Since most of the relevant sayings have been uttered in private to the disciples, it seems likely it is Judas who has fed the authorities with appropriate evidence which they can use against Jesus when the time comes.

# Why did he do it?

It has always seemed incredible that a man who has devoted a year or more of his life to following Jesus could suddenly turn against him in this way. Few have been able to believe that a cash payment would alone be enough to motivate such a radical decision. Beyond that we are in the area of conjecture.

One interesting fact is that Judas' name, Iscariot, may indicate that he came from a town, Keriot, in southern Judea. If so, that would probably mean that he was the only non-Galilean among the twelve. So he may have come to feel out of place in this Galilean movement, and the more so when the group has come down to Judea, and the Galilean crowds have welcomed 'their' prophet into the capital. So perhaps there is an element of racial prejudice in Judas' decision.

But it is likely that there is a more fundamental reason that that. As they have journeyed towards Jerusalem Jesus has again and again made it quite plain to his disciples that he has no intention, as many had hoped, of leading a movement to restore Israel's national independence; his mission is not to lead his people to victory but to be rejected and die. Peter's remonstrance against such an idea (8:32) would have been echoed by the other disciples, and they have followed him reluctantly and with bewilderment.

If Judas originally joined the movement for motives of high-minded patriotism, he will have watched with dismay as Jesus has stubbornly rejected any such mission. And now in Jerusalem Jesus has made matters worse by actually attacking the temple itself, the very symbol of national pride, and daring to predict its destruction. Judas' desertion would then have been the result of disillusionment: this is not the sort of movement he had thought he was joining. His approach to the priests would then be partly an attempt to save his own skin while there is still time; but it might also arise from a genuine conviction that Jesus has embarked on a dangerous and unpatriotic course, and must be stopped before he does any more harm.

## FOR MEDITATION

*If you think you are standing, watch out that you do not fall.*
**1 Corinthians 10:12**

# 90 The Passover meal

## Old Passover and new

Jesus died at the festival of Passover, and it was at a Passover meal on the night before he died that he instituted the central act of Christian worship, the Lord's supper. The Passover is itself a commemorative meal, celebrating Israel's original liberation from slavery in Egypt. It was through this act of God, and under the leadership of Moses, that Israel became a nation. Now a new Passover meal, under a new leader, marks the foundation of a people of God which is no longer national but international, the people of the new covenant.

And at the heart of the Passover ritual is death, the death of the lamb, whose blood on the doorposts kept safe the houses of the Israelites when the firstborn of Egypt were being killed. Now blood will again be shed, the blood not of a sacrificial lamb but of the Son of God, by whose death 'many' will be saved.

## The Last Supper

In the light of all this symbolism of the Passover, and its significance for what is now taking place, it is no wonder that Jesus has made careful preparations for this last meal with his disciples. The meeting with the man carrying a jar of water is not a coincidence, but, like the finding of the donkey for the ride into Jerusalem, has been planned in advance, for the room is already prepared and waiting for them. There is at least one houseowner in Jerusalem who can be relied on to help Jesus even in these threatening days. Here the group who have spent so much time together in the last year or two will share a last meal together, and Jesus wants to make sure that it is a special occasion. In years to come they will remember and pass on every detail of it, as they 'do this in remembrance of me' (1 Corinthians 11:23–26).

# The cuckoo in the nest

But first there is an important matter to be dealt with. The group of twelve is soon to be cruelly broken up, and Jesus does not want the rest of them to be taken by surprise. They must be made to realize that there is a traitor among them, and that Jesus himself knows it, even though he will do nothing to stop him. He tells them clearly that one of the twelve will betray him, but does not say which one it will be. If he had identified the traitor no doubt Peter and the others would have made sure that Judas did not leave the room to go about his deadly business. By not identifying Judas, Jesus, not for the only time, deliberately lets slip an opportunity to prevent the course of events which will bring him to the cross. This is what he has come to Jerusalem for, and he will not now try to avoid it.

The disciples' anguished question, 'Surely, not I?', is probably not just a rhetorical question. After the bewildering experiences of recent weeks, and their constant failure to be in tune with Jesus' way of thinking, probably none of them could be quite sure that he would not let the side down in the end. But the form of the question is one which, as the grammarians say, 'expects the answer No'; none of them can really believe that he would fall so low. Mark does not say whether Judas asked the same question, in the same form. I wonder!

## PRAYER

*Lord, may we bring you our fears and our failures as well as our faith and our love for you, secure in the knowledge that you know us better than we know ourselves.*

# 91
# Startling symbolism

The Passover meal consisted of a series of courses interspersed by cups of wine (four in all), and for each course and each cup there were appropriate words of blessing and explanation repeated by the head of the family. Jesus, as head of the 'family' of his disciples, also utters blessings and adds words of explanation, but his explanations are startlingly new and disturbing. This is a Passover with a difference!

## This is my body; this is my blood

Whatever else the disciples may yet have understood, they cannot miss the essential point that Jesus is enacting before them his own death. Even if they have not yet taken his predictions seriously, there can now be no doubt that he has meant what he has said. His body is about to be broken, and his blood poured out. The bread and wine are thus symbols of death.

But in inviting them to eat the bread and drink the wine Jesus is adding another level to the symbolism. The death he is enacting is to be one in which they are in some way to participate. The broken body and shed blood are to be food and drink for his people. The imagery is shocking: are Christians to be cannibals? But by now we know better than to assume that Jesus' sayings are always to be taken dead literally. Eating and drinking are the basis of life, and Jesus is to be the basis of the disciple's life. The bread and wine which symbolize his death are the disciple's sustenance, for his death is the source of our life.

## A covenant... for many

The words over the cup are full of Old Testament echoes. At Mount Sinai, when Israel came out of Egypt to become a nation under Moses, God made a covenant with them, and it was this covenant which was the basis of their status as God's chosen people. It was sealed with the blood of sacrifices, and Moses proclaimed 'See the blood of the covenant...' (Exodus 24:8). Now another sacrifice will seal a new covenant, and the people of God will be reborn. And the words 'for many' are an echo of Isaiah 53:11, 12 (as we have already seen in 10:45), the prophecy of the servant of God whose mission it is to suffer and die for the salvation of his people. So the death that Jesus is about to undergo is not a mistake or a disaster, but the means to the salvation of his people, the people of the new covenant.

## Looking forward

Verses 22–24 speak of death, but that death is not the end, and in verse 25 Jesus is already looking forward beyond the cross to the new life of the kingdom of God. This is his last meal and his last drink on earth, but soon there will be new wine to enjoy. Jesus is thinking probably of the messianic banquet which all Jews looked forward to enjoying in the last days. That time is now fast approaching, and soon Jesus and his disciples will be able to celebrate together.

So the final Passover meal is in fact but a foretaste of what is to come. There will be death tomorrow, but through that death there will be life for ever. As Christians today share the bread and wine of the Lord's supper, they do so with due solemnity indeed, for it is their Lord's death which they are remembering, but also with thanksgiving (which is what 'eucharist' means) for the life which that death has achieved.

### FOR MEDITATION

*In what ways might it enrich our understanding of our worship at the holy communion if we were able to enter more fully into the experience and understanding of the disciples at that last supper in Jerusalem?*

# Trouble ahead

The sense of impending disaster was already strong at the Passover meal, as Jesus not only enacted symbolically his own imminent death but also predicted that one of his twelve closest associates would turn against him. But in these verses which follow the account of the meal the screw is turned even tighter: not only one of them, but *all*, will desert him in the end!

## The Mount of Olives

The Mount of Olives is the hillside which faces Jerusalem across the narrow valley of the Kidron. Many Passover pilgrims would be camping out in this area. Bethany, where Jesus has been staying since coming to Jerusalem, is on the other side of the hill, but for this night he is not going back to Bethany, but staying closer to the city. Gethsemane is the name of a plot of land, probably an olive orchard, on the slope opposite the city, and this is where (as Judas already knows) Jesus and his disciples are going for the night. The 'hymn' referred to in verse 26 will be the Hallel psalm traditionally sung at the Passover season. With that their Passover meal is over, and they go out to face the terrible events for which Jesus has so long been preparing them.

## The scattering of the sheep

But all that preparation has not been enough. Jesus knows that they will not be able to stand the pressure which is soon to come upon them all. He knows it because he knows them too well. But he knows it also because the prophecy of Zechariah (that same book from which he drew the model for his triumphant ride into Jerusalem) has predicted it. Throughout these final hours in Jerusalem there is a recurrent theme of the fulfilment of prophecy. These are not random, unscripted events, but the outworking of a pattern long ago perceived and set down by God's spokesmen for the last days. Among Zechariah's prophecies the vision of a rejected and stricken shepherd is one of the most memorable, and Jesus knows that that is to be his role.

The disciples are not yet so clear-sighted. All of them (except Judas, presumably, who has already gone about his business) believe that they will be able to stand the strain. Their loyalty is unquestioned, but its strength is as yet untested, and when the test comes it will fail. Peter, as usual, is both the spokesman for the group, and the man who is confident in his own loyalty and strength of character. But his reward for such gallantry is to be given his own personal prediction of betrayal; before many hours have passed the cock will crow, and he will remember.

## Back to Galilee

Yet among this overwhelming sense of gloom and foreboding, Jesus' mind is still, as it was at the Passover meal (v. 25), not only on the more immediate future, but on the ultimate outcome. Beyond the cross, he can see the resurrection; beyond the rejection and death in Jerusalem is the triumphant return to Galilee. There, in the familiar hills, he looks forward to a rendezvous with the eleven disciples, who will have put their temporary failure behind them, and will be ready for a new beginning, back in the province where it all began so hopefully all those months ago. It is astonishing that a man who knows he is about to die can speak so calmly of a new beginning, and his disciples seem still to be quite unable to grasp what he is talking about. But by now we should be getting used to being astonished by Jesus!

### PRAYER
*Lord, you know us better than we know ourselves. Keep us from being too confident in our own resources, and help us instead to listen to you and to find our strength in you.*

# Gethsemane

Here we are on holy ground, privileged to join Peter, James and John in sharing one of the most poignant and personal moments in Jesus' life on earth. More than once Mark has told us about Jesus praying, but now we come closer and hear the actual words of the Son of God as he pleads with his Father. And they are astonishing words.

## Jesus in distress

After the apparently calm way in which Jesus has spoken repeatedly to his disciples about the fate which awaits him in Jerusalem, it is sobering to witness now his extreme agitation as the time comes closer and the prospect becomes more real. Some Christians have mistakenly pictured Jesus as a sort of superman whose humanity was only skin-deep, and who sailed untroubled through the experiences of life, and death, on earth. Mark will not allow any such fantasy. Jesus is well aware of what is soon to happen to him, and the prospect horrifies him.

It is a mark of the depth of his suffering, and of the reality of his human character, that in this time of crisis he wants and needs human companionship. Peter, James and John are there not merely as spectators, but for the support they ought to be able to give to Jesus in his distress.

## Remove this cup

Before they fell asleep the disciples heard enough to know the gist of Jesus' prayer. They heard and remembered the confident way in which Jesus addressed God by the familiar term 'Abba', a degree of closeness to God which other Jews at that time did not presume to claim. But even more memorably they heard the Son of God, whose clear predictions of his coming suffering and death they had had to come to terms with, now pleading to be 'let off the hook'. The 'cup' was an Old Testament image for destined suffering and judgment (remember 10:38); now that Jesus looks into it he is appalled by what he sees.

We cannot hope to enter fully into the thoughts and emotions of the Son of God as he comes face to face with what his Father has called him to undergo. Many a hero has resolutely faced physical death, but there is more to Jesus' revulsion than that. We have been given some clues in his words about the purpose of his death: 'a ransom for many' (10:45), 'blood poured out for many' (14:24), the role of the Servant of God who dies for the sins of his people. We shall see something of the horror of what this means in Jesus' cry from the cross in 15:34.

But with the horror goes the acceptance of the Father's will, all the more amazing because Jesus now knows just what it will mean: 'Not what I want, but what you want.'

## The flesh is weak

In contrast with Jesus' hard-won readiness to suffer is the disciples' total unreadiness. Exhausted by the bewildering pace of events, they cannot even stay awake to give Jesus the support he needs. Yet they need to pray for themselves (v. 38) as well as for him. In a few moments they will be, almost literally, caught napping.

**PRAYER**

*'Abba, Father, not what I want but what you want.'*

191

# 94

# Betrayal and arrest

The arrest of Jesus is carried out by an armed 'crowd', not specifically described as either soldiers or police, but sent out with the authority of 'the chief priests, the scribes, and the elders'. Mark has used this full listing of the component groups of the Sanhedrin before when he wishes to emphasize the official nature of the opposition to Jesus (8:31; 11:27; see also 14:53). This is not a Roman action, but the Sanhedrin exercising its delegated power to control the internal affairs of the Jewish community, and so it will be to the Sanhedrin, not to the Roman governor, that Jesus will be taken.

## The kiss of Judas

Judas has fulfilled his bargain and has brought the arresting party through the darkness to the right one among the many pilgrim groups camping out on the Mount of Olives. His final, famous act of betrayal, to identify Jesus with a kiss, seems hardly necessary, since Jesus has become a well-known figure during the last few days as he has taught publicly in the temple, but perhaps in the darkness the Jerusalem crowd might find it hard to single out the right man among these Galilean strangers.

## Who is in charge?

Jesus apparently offers no resistance when he is arrested, and when 'one of those who stood near' attempts to fight for him he does not seem to encourage the attempt. His rebuke in verse 48 is addressed to the arresting party, but it implies that there is no place for weapons to be used on either side. He is not a desperado but a peaceful religious teacher.

So Jesus is the unresisting victim of an armed crowd. And yet there is a tone of authority in his rebuke, and his final words, 'Let the scriptures be fulfilled', show that he has not been taken by surprise, and is now ready for what is to come. If Jesus had wished to avoid arrest, he need not have gone to Gethsemane that night. He is being arrested because that is what he has accepted as the Father's will, not because he is helpless.

## The scattering of the sheep

Jesus' prediction in verse 27 is now fulfilled. Perhaps the disciples feel they have little option: if Jesus does not wish to resist his arrest, what else is there for them to do? But the language is not of an orderly withdrawal, but of panic-stricken flight to save their own skins, and the vivid little story of the naked young man shows that they had reason to be afraid. Bewildered by the way things have developed since they came to Jerusalem, demoralized by Judas' desertion, and now thrown by Jesus' determination not to resist arrest, they quickly turn and run. We can only guess what would be going through their minds as they disappear among the trees.

### FOR MEDITATION

*Think how the arrest of Jesus must have seemed to the various people in Gethsemane that night: the armed crowd, Judas, the disciples, the young man who ran away.*

# 95 Before the Sanhedrin

Mark carefully sets the scene at the high priest's house on a double stage: Jesus before the full council of the Sanhedrin (v. 53; note again the full listing of the dignitaries) and Peter out in the courtyard among the servants (v. 54). As the spotlight falls first on the one stage and then (vv. 66–72) on the other, we shall see a striking contrast between the two men under pressure.

## False testimony

Mark clearly does not want us to think of this as a fair and impartial trial. The aim is, quite simply, 'to put him to death'. The verdict is already decided, and the only problem is how to find suitable evidence to support it. But it seems that the authorities are anxious to ensure that due process of law is seen to have been carried out. Jewish law demanded that a defendant should have the right to be heard, and that any evidence for the prosecution must be sustained by two independent witnesses under cross-examination. There is in this case, apparently, no shortage of willing witnesses, but their act has not been adequately prepared, and under cross-examination they fail to establish their charges: 'their testimony did not agree'.

## A new temple

The failure to agree is surprising when we notice the one specific charge which Mark records and declares to be false (vv. 57–59). Jesus' cavalier attitude to the temple has been one of the main reasons for the hostility of the Jerusalem authorities. In both words and actions he has declared his belief that it is no longer fulfilling its purpose as the focus of Israel's religious life. In the hearing of his disciples, if not more openly, Jesus has actually predicted that the temple will soon be totally destroyed (13:2), and Judas will by now have had time to pass on this incriminating statement to the authorities. True, as far as our records go, Jesus has not said that he will himself destroy the temple or that it will be replaced with another, but the charge is sufficiently close to the tenor of his words and deeds to be a damaging one, if only they could get their 'witnesses' to agree on the words he has used. We shall see in 15:29 that this charge against Jesus stuck in the popular mind, even if it could not be made to stand up in court.

But while Mark records the charge as, technically, false, he does not want us to miss its theological significance. By including the phrases 'made with hands' and 'not made with hands' he underlines the contrast which is important throughout the New Testament between a religion based on external, man-made structures and a religion of the heart and life, between a community which finds its focus in a building and one which knows no such restriction. While they failed in their charge, these witnesses in fact spoke truer than they knew.

## No case to answer?

Jesus' silence may be purely pragmatic: there is, as yet, no case to answer and therefore no need to exercise his right to speak in his own defence. When it is time to speak he will not be reluctant to do so. But his silence infuriates the high priest, and leaves him with no choice but to invite the prisoner to incriminate himself.

But Mark may also want us to remember what Isaiah said about the Servant of the Lord: 'He was oppressed, and he was afflicted, yet he did not open his mouth; like a lamb that is led to the slaughter, and like a sheep that before its shearers is silent, so he did not open his mouth' (Isaiah 53:7).

**PRAYER**

*Lord, as you faced injustice and dishonour for us, may we be prepared also to be abused for you. Help us to know when to speak and when to be silent.*

# 96 The secret is unveiled

## 'Are you the Messiah?'

The high priest's question is not so much a change of subject as it may seem. To claim, as Jesus is alleged to have claimed, the right to replace the temple was, in effect, to claim to be the Messiah, since the Messiah was expected to restore the temple. But by phrasing it as directly as this, the high priest goes to the heart of the question of Jesus' authority to act and speak in so radical a way.

And by linking the title of Messiah with that of 'Son of God' ('Son of the Blessed One' is a Jewish way of saying the same thing without pronouncing the sacred name of God) he takes up the even more audacious claim which Judas must have told him about (12:6; 13:32), and which the three disciples may not have been able to keep secret when they came down from the mountain (9:7,9). So here is a chance for Jesus to clear up any doubt about who he thinks he is.

## An open confession

While Jesus might still have been mistaken for a political liberator, he kept his role as Messiah a secret. But now, on trial for his life before the nation's leaders, no such misunderstanding is possible. The moment has come for Jesus to reveal publicly who he is, and he does it in a ringing declaration which goes far beyond the terms of the high priest's question. The 'I am' is clear enough, but Jesus does not leave it at that.

When Peter first hailed Jesus as the Messiah, Jesus immediately went on to speak of himself instead as the Son of man (8:29-31). Now he does the same thing, but this time instead of speaking of the suffering of the Son of man he speaks of his glory. He uses again the words of Daniel 7:13, the vision of the 'one like a son of man coming with the clouds of heaven' to be enthroned in the presence of God as lord of all nations for ever. Combined with this are the words of Psalm 110:1 (see above on 12:35-37) about sitting at God's right hand. The two prophecies together declare that the prisoner in the dock is none other than God's designated king, and those who now presume to sit in judgment over him will live to see it. Here, as in 8:38—9:1 and in 13:26, 30, Jesus expects the vision of Daniel to be visibly fulfilled within the generation (see comments on those passages for how this may have been fulfilled).

## Blasphemy

To claim to be the Messiah was not in itself blasphemous—if it was true! But Jesus' judges have decided in advance that it is not true, and combined with his presumptuous language about sitting at God's right hand it is more than enough for a verdict. Witnesses are now irrelevant; they have heard it for themselves. This is what they have been trying for, and the solemn court proceedings now degenerate into cruel parody. There was a belief that the Messiah would be identified by his ability to recognize those who touched him when blindfolded. It is not hard to imagine the gusto with which they put this pretender to the test.

### FOR MEDITATION

*Compare the authority of the Sanhedrin with the authority of Jesus, the Son of man. If you had been there as a member of the Sanhedrin, what would you have made of verse 62, uttered by a helpless prisoner on trial for his life?*

# 97 The witness who failed

We noted that in verses 53–54 Mark has set up this part of his drama on a double stage. The effect is to allow us to watch a tale of two witnesses. So far the spotlight has been on Jesus, called upon to testify to his divine calling in the highest court in the land, and he has done so decisively and with courage. Now we return to the courtyard where Peter sits among the servants. How will he match up to the test?

## At least he was there

Before we rake over Peter's notorious failure, we should notice that he is by now the only disciple who is anywhere near Jesus. Jesus' prediction that all the disciples would desert him (v. 27) has been literally fulfilled (v. 50), all except for Peter. Peter, who had the temerity to contradict Jesus and to insist on his own loyalty to death (vv. 29–31), has so far proved as good as his word. He is in the high priest's courtyard, and he is alone. This dogged loyalty will make his ultimate failure look all the more miserable, but at least we should give him the credit for having come so far. Only Peter denied Jesus— but only Peter had put himself in a position to face the test.

## The turning of the screw

In the three challenges to Peter there is a steady increase in the pressure put upon him. First comes a private challenge from just one servant-girl, which is relatively easily brushed off. Then she makes her suspicions public, and that is more serious. But a further denial still does not get Peter off the hook, and the whole group come back at him with the additional evidence of his tell-tale Galilean accent. So Peter has to resort to drastic measures to escape the net which seems to be closing round him: 'he began to curse, and he swore an oath'. The Greek verb 'curse' normally has an object: it is to curse *someone*, not just to utter profanities. Did Peter actually go to the length of uttering a curse upon Jesus, to make it clear that he could not be his follower? Mark does not make it explicit, but that is the natural implication of the word he uses.

## The cock crows

Under the pressure of the moment Peter has apparently forgotten all about Jesus' warning, and his own brash self-confidence on the Mount of Olives before Jesus was arrested. The crowing of the cock brings it all back, and Peter breaks down. We can imagine the self-disgust which the memory would evoke, the utter sense of failure and humiliation. But worse than that is the knowledge that he has betrayed the man who has come to mean more to him even than his own family. And worse still, this man is the Son of God. Peter, who was so proud to confess Jesus as his Messiah at Caesarea Philippi, has fallen right into the trap which Jesus had warned him of immediately afterwards: 'Those who are ashamed of me and of my words in this adulterous and sinful generation...' (8:38). No wonder he wept.

But this is not the last time we shall hear of Peter. When Jesus has risen from the dead he will send a message to 'his disciples and Peter' (16:7). For this special disciple there is not only a special failure, but also a special message from the master he has betrayed. His tears of sorrow are the prelude to restoration. There is hope even for a Peter. (It is interesting to notice the difference between Peter and Judas, both traitors, but one whose treachery under the pressure of the moment was not an irrevocable disaster.)

**PRAYER**

*Lord, you know that the flesh is weak. Help us not so much to condemn Peter as to learn from his experience.*

# 98

# Enter Pontius Pilate

It was one thing for a Jewish court to decide on the death penalty, but quite another to implement it. Under the direct Roman rule which had now been imposed in Judea the right to pronounce the death penalty was reserved to the Roman governor alone. So to achieve an execution they must secure a conviction also before Pontius Pilatus, the Prefect of Judea. And that was not necessarily going to be easy.

## Pontius Pilatus

The man who represented Roman power in Judea through the time of Jesus' public activity was a mean-minded and brutal official, by no means typical of Roman government at its best. Contemporary records mention no less than five occasions on which his insensitive handling of situations led to serious unrest among his Jewish or Samaritan subjects, three times resulting in a massacre while a fourth was narrowly averted. In the end, some years after Jesus appeared before him, he was removed from office for misgovernment. So the Jewish authorities could certainly not count on an official rubber stamp on their verdict. It was not in Pilate's character to be nice to the Jews.

## 'King of the Jews'

To tell Pilate that Jesus claimed to be the Messiah and the Son of God, or that he had committed blasphemy, would not cut much ice. These were not crimes against the state, and would be of little interest to a pagan governor. But the title Messiah was easily translated into a title with a much more sinister political ring to it, 'King of the Jews'. It was on the charge of claiming this title, then, that the Jewish leaders brought their prisoner before the governor early in the morning, and it would be under this title that, before many hours had passed, Jesus would hang on the cross.

# 'Have you no answer?'

The silence of Jesus which had so exasperated the high priest is now repeated before Pilate, and Mark emphasizes it even more strongly. True, Jesus does respond to the first question, '*Are* you the King of the Jews?', but his answer gives little away: 'You say so'! This phrase occurs a number of times in the Gospels, and it seems generally to be a guarded 'Yes'—guarded in the sense that while the words used are in a real sense correct, they are easily misunderstood. Jesus *is* the King of the Jews: that was what he had enacted when he rode into Jerusalem. But he is a king on a much wider stage than merely Jewish national politics, the Son of man who will soon be seated at the right hand of God as sovereign over all nations. To turn this sublime destiny into a local political intrigue, as surely Pilate must have understood by the phrase 'King of the Jews', was to miss the point completely. So Jesus' answer probably means 'That is how you put it, but the truth is very different from what you are thinking.'

And after that he has no more to say. His next words will be the terrible cry from the cross. Had he wished, he could have mounted a strong and probably convincing defence, and Pilate might well have held out against the Jewish pressure. But again Jesus refuses the opportunity to deflect the course of events which he knows to be his Father's will.

## FOR MEDITATION

*Think how easy it is for people to miss the point about Jesus. What are the sort of ways in which people today jump to wrong conclusions about him? How would you explain Jesus' kingship to someone who did not have a background knowledge of the Old and New Testaments?*

99

# Barabbas

### 'The insurrection'

Barabbas was not just a common criminal. He was a 'rebel', who had been involved in an 'insurrection'. We have no other record of this particular uprising against the Roman occupation, but it need not surprise us: several such incidents are recorded in the turbulent years between the imposition of Roman rule and the final and cata-strophic revolt in AD66 which led to the destruction of the temple. And Barabbas was, probably, the leader of this earlier revolt, since it is he whom the crowd now want to have released. He was, therefore, a patriotic leader, a popular hero, of the sort many may well have hoped that Jesus would agree to become. He has the popular sup-port of a Robin Hood.

### The amnesty

Pilate is a pragmatist. He has apparently been sufficiently impressed by Jesus to feel that he is not a political danger, and so is trying to avoid sentencing an innocent man. But the pressure from the crowd is building up, and the last thing a governor wants is a rioting crowd at the sensitive time of the Passover festival. So the traditional amnesty seems a convenient way to avoid an unnecessary conviction. Why not substitute this newly-accused 'King of the Jews' for the other nationalist leader. The fact that Jesus is as yet uncondemned and therefore needs no amnesty, while Barabbas is a convicted crim-inal, does not seem to bother him.

Unfortunately, he has miscalculated. It is Barabbas whom the peo-ple of Jerusalem recognize as their sort of hero. This supposed 'King of the Jews' is a stranger from Galilee, and he has shown no inclina-tion to take up the patriotic cause. They are not to be fobbed off with a pseudo-revolutionary.

# 'Crucify him'

People sometimes express surprise that a crowd who welcomed Jesus with shouts of 'Hosanna' only a few days before could so quickly turn against him. But that is to miss the point completely. Those who welcomed Jesus into the city were the Passover pilgrims arriving with him from Galilee, and Mark has given us no reason to think that the people of Jerusalem joined in the celebrations; indeed Matthew makes it clear that they took a very different view of this Galilean prophet (Matthew 21:10–11). But the crowd outside the governor's headquarters early on this festival morning are the people of Jerusalem, and they have no doubt which 'king' they want: not this Galilean teacher but their own Barabbas, who has already proved his patriotic credentials through 'the insurrection'.

What is surprising and chilling, however, is to hear a Jewish crowd calling for the barbaric Roman punishment of crucifixion to be imposed on any Jew, however unwelcome his political stance. But they have been under Roman rule long enough to know that this is the way the Romans deal with sedition: whether it is Barabbas or Jesus, this will be the fate of the one who is not released. And the chief priests are determined to be rid of Jesus, even if this cruel form of execution is the only way to do it. So let him be crucified.

Pilate is not a man of principle, and he gives way to the pressure. He adds his own characteristically sadistic touch by having the condemned man flogged before execution, a brutal flogging with leather thongs which was often in itself fatal.

## FOR MEDITATION

*He was wounded for our transgressions,*
*crushed for our iniquities;*
*upon him was the punishment that made us whole,*
*and by his bruises we are healed.*

**Isaiah 53:5**

# 100 Homage to the 'king'

## In the hands of the Romans

Even among the Jewish people Jesus has been subjected to cruelty and abuse both from the members of the Sanhedrin and from their (Jewish) guards (14:65). But now he is in the hands of the Romans, and they too will have their turn. For them there is not the same religious motive of horror at his 'blasphemy'. But for a group of bored soldiers of the occupying forces it would be a welcome diversion to have in their power the so-called 'King of the Jews'. If, like many Romans at the time, they had no great love for the Jewish people and their strange religion, it would come naturally to poke fun at a popular Jewish leader and religious teacher, now out of favour. And a group of ordinary soldiers would do it with no great refinement or delicacy.

## 'Hail, King of the Jews'

It may not be much of an exaggeration to say that 'the whole cohort' (which would at full strength be 600 men) gathered together for a mock parade before the 'King'; none of them would want to miss the fun. Clearly a king must have the proper symbols of royalty, and so they are provided. The 'purple cloak' is probably a soldier's red cape made to do duty for the imperial purple, and the 'reed' with which they strike him would represent the royal sceptre. For a crown, they improvise a coronet made of 'thorns' (perhaps the long spikes that grow at the base of a date-palm leaf), to imitate the crowns worn by oriental rulers which had rays like those of the sun. And in this parody of splendour they kneel and pay homage to the captive 'king'.

But sheer mockery is not enough for them, and the homage degenerates into horseplay. Following so soon after a severe flogging the physical pain must have been been extreme, and the humiliating appearance of the bedraggled 'king' would only add to their enjoyment. So Jesus' words on the way to Jerusalem are coming to very literal and terrible fulfilment: 'They will hand him over to the

Gentiles; they will mock him, and spit upon him, and flog him, and kill him.' Now it is all happening. Jesus himself has become the passive focus of a relentless course of events which will soon bring him inevitably to the cross.

## What sort of a king?

For the soldiers, no doubt, the situation was simple enough. Here was a man who had had the foolhardiness to challenge the might of Rome and to attempt to lead his people to liberation. He had failed, as all such insurgents were bound to fail, and now he must accept the consequences. The label 'King of the Jews' said it all.

But there is a telling irony in Mark's account. None of this is true of Jesus. Others may have wanted him to be such a 'king', but he has consistently set himself against the role of the popular liberator. Yet here is he, who repudiated such a kingship, condemned to suffer for it, while Barabbas, who hoped to be just such a leader, is going free. And yet Jesus is a king as well, the Son of man who is to be enthroned at the right hand of God, with a universal sovereignty which makes any mere Jewish kingship look very pale. And that kingship is to be over all nations: the one whom the Gentile soldiers are mocking is not merely the king of the Jews, but their king as well.

### PRAYER

*Help us to offer you true homage, Lord, and hasten the time when all nations will recognize and worship you as their true king.*

Crucifixion was a particularly cruel form of execution reserved normally for slaves and for political insurgents. The Roman writer Cicero called it 'the most cruel and revolting punishment' and the Jew Josephus called it 'the most pitiable of deaths'. A crucified person would hang in agony for hours, sometimes days, before finally dying. And it was a horribly public form of execution, designed as a deterrent to passers-by. Human nature being what it is, Golgotha, the public gibbet, would be a place where many would gather.

## Carrying the cross

It was probably the cross-beam which was carried, normally by the criminal himself, to be fixed to an upright post on arrival at the place of execution. After the flogging and the ill-treatment by the soldiers Jesus is in no state to carry the beam himself, and a stranger who just happens to be in the wrong place at the wrong time is given the dubious honour. Jesus had talked about his disciples taking up their own cross and following him, but now there are no disciples to be found to carry his cross.

But Mark curiously mentions the names of Simon's two sons. Is this perhaps because they would be known to his readers? If so that means that even if Simon was a complete stranger at the time, his family later became members of the church. Was it this day's forced labour which set Simon's family on a new course? (One of the sons may perhaps have been the 'Alexander, son of Simon' whose funeral inscription was found in a tomb near Jerusalem probably belonging to a Jewish family from Cyrene.)

## Crucifixion

The narcotic drink to dull the pain was kindly meant, but Jesus refuses it, determined to undergo the ordeal in full consciousness. Mark gives no details of the fastening to the cross. He mentions rather the offer of drugged wine and the casting of lots for Jesus' clothes because in these minor details of the scene Christians had come to recognize the fulfilment of Scripture: see Psalms 22:18 and 69:21, two psalms from which several echoes are found in the passion story.

Mark's mention of nine o'clock in the morning is a problem, since John 19:14 has Jesus still before Pilate at noon, and the other Gospels more easily agree with that timing. For Mark Jesus remained alive on the cross for at least six hours, for the others probably not much more than three hours. John's detailed account inspires confidence, and Mark may have confused the time of the trial with that of the crucifixion.

## In bad company

The 'bandits' may well have been some of Barabbas' associates in 'the insurrection', since the same term is used by Josephus to describe political insurgents. So Jesus, who has refused the temptation to lead a political movement, dies in the company of revolutionaries. And the placard above his head bears the title which was used against him at his trial and was the basis of his condemnation, 'The King of the Jews'. We have thought before of the irony of Jesus being executed under such a title. The presence of the two freedom fighters on either side of him merely compounds the irony, and underlines the depth of popular, and indeed official, misunderstanding of what Jesus' mission has been all about.

### FOR MEDITATION

*If you had been an uninvolved passer-by at Golgotha that day, what would you have seen and felt? Would you have had any idea of the significance of what was happening? Why did God allow it to be like this?*

# 102
# Mockery

## Rejection

When Jesus foretold his coming suffering in Jerusalem he included along with his physical suffering and death the prospect of being 'rejected' (8:31). For the disciples this must surely have been one of the most terrible and incomprehensible aspects of his predictions. How could the Messiah of Israel be rejected by the very people God is sending him to save?

In these few verses that rejection is graphically portrayed. We have seen the mockery of the Gentile soldiers, but perhaps that could be excused—they knew no better. But now it is Jews who join the mocking chorus. And they are Jews of all classes, the ordinary passers-by (v. 29), the religious authorities (v. 31) and even the patriots who hang on the crosses beside him (v. 32). And there is not a disciple in sight.

## Paradoxical truth

As the proverb says, 'There's many a true word spoken in jest.' The titles which are now thrown at Jesus in mockery are ones in which we, Mark's readers, can see with hindsight some of the most vital truths about Jesus and why he was there on the cross.

He is the 'destroyer and rebuilder of the temple'. There is, they assume, no prospect of that now that he has been hung up to die. But we have seen already that one result of Jesus' death on the cross will be to hasten the end of the old temple, and to set in motion the formation of a new temple, 'not made with hands', to take its place. Even as he dies this drastic change in the divine purpose will be vividly symbolized in the tearing of the temple curtain (v. 38).

He claimed to be 'the Messiah, the King of Israel', but now that he is dying his pretensions have, they suppose, been shown to be hollow. And yet Jesus has been teaching his disciples that his suffering and death is in fact at the very centre of his messianic mission. It is not failure, but his crowning achievement. It is the route he must take to his future glory, seated at the right hand of God, where he will be the king not only of Israel but of all nations. All this we have learned already, if we have listened to Jesus' private teaching of his disciples. But those who are standing by the cross have no inkling of this truth.

He is the one who claimed to save others, yet he cannot save himself. But the cross is in fact the very means of that salvation, to die as a ransom for many, to shed his 'blood of the covenant' for many. If Jesus could have 'saved himself', by avoiding the cross (the temptation he fought and overcame in Gethsemane), he would in fact have forfeited his ability to save others.

But to see these depths in the meaning of Jesus' crucifixion you need to have absorbed his startling teaching, so extraordinary that even his closest disciples have not yet been able to grasp it. No wonder the bystanders at the cross knew nothing of it, and used as mocking insults the very truths on which Jesus' mission depended.

## 'As it is written'

Several times we have heard Jesus say or imply that what is going to happen to him is in fulfilment of the scriptures (8:31 'must'; 9:12; 14:21, 27, 49). As he has tried to explain why he must die he has echoed the words of Isaiah 53 (10:45; 14:24). Now Mark again draws in the testimony of Psalm 22, which he has already alluded to in verse 24. A central theme of that psalm is the mockery endured by the godly sufferer, and in verse 29 he again echoes that psalm: 'All who see me mock at me; they make mouths at me, they shake their heads' (Psalm 22:7). Soon we shall hear Jesus himself expressing his deepest agony in the words of that same psalm (v. 34). The scriptures are indeed being fulfilled.

**PRAYER**

*Sometimes it causes me to tremble, tremble, tremble;*
*Were you there when they crucified my Lord?*

# 103 Alone on the cross

If to overhear Jesus praying in Gethsemane was to tread on holy ground, surely here we venture into the Holy of Holies, as we hear the only words of Jesus on the cross which Mark has recorded. Indeed, these are the only words of Jesus in this Gospel after his enigmatic 'You say so' before Pilate. Through the crowd's hostility, his condemnation and flogging, the soldiers' mockery and the extreme pain of being hung on the cross, Jesus has been a silent, passive victim. But now he breaks his silence in one powerful, appalling cry of desolation, which so impressed itself on those who heard it that they remembered and passed it on in the original Aramaic.

## In the dark

Darkness at midday cannot have been caused by a natural eclipse of the sun at Passover time, because then the moon is full. However it was caused, it is an expression of God's anger, as in Amos 8:9 and in the plagues of Egypt (Exodus 10:22). It is also a symbol of the darkness into which Jesus himself now enters, the darkness of abandonment by his Father.

The words are the opening line of Psalm 22, and the whole psalm, as we have seen, spells out the agony of the godly sufferer, at the mercy of his mocking enemies. But the words Jesus draws from that psalm are perhaps, for him, the most terrible of all. For the Son of God to be abandoned by his Father is the ultimate, unthinkable horror. This is, significantly, the only time in all the Gospels when Jesus does not use the term 'Father' to address God in prayer. A darkness has come between them.

It would be impertinent for us to try to penetrate the nature of the relationship between Jesus and his Father in order to analyse what such a separation might mean. But Jesus' own words about giving his life as a ransom for many perhaps take us as far as we dare go, by reminding us of the role of the Servant of God: 'the Lord has laid on him the iniquity of us all'. We may well believe that when Jesus shrunk from the cross in Gethsemane it was the prospect of this sin-bearing rather than only the physical suffering of the cross which appalled him. And now it has happened, and he is alone, abandoned not only by his earthly friends but even by his Father.

## Enter Elijah?

After the numbing mystery of Jesus' words the reaction of the bystanders is a pathetic anticlimax. They hear the name 'Eloi, Eloi', and mistake it for Elijah. Elijah, as we have seen, was expected to return in the last days, and some Jews came to think of him as a sort of heavenly superman figure who would be available to rescue God's people in times of extreme need. But probably the crowd at Golgotha take this idea no more seriously than the great titles they have already flung against Jesus on the cross, and the attempt to give Jesus a drink to keep him going until Elijah comes will merely have added to the ribald humour of the occasion.

### FOR MEDITATION

*Read Psalm 22, and think why these words may have come to Jesus' mind at such a time.*

# 104
# The end?

## The death of Jesus

Most victims of crucifixion lingered on in pain for many hours, and gradually lost consciousness. Jesus' death is very different. Now that he has borne the ultimate horror of his Father's withdrawal from him, his work is done, and his death comes suddenly and with a loud cry. It is as if he is deliberately letting go. John 19:30 tells us that that loud cry was one of triumph, 'I have done it!'

The temple had two great curtains, one covering the entrance to the Holy Place, where only the priests could go to offer incense, and one separating off the Holy of Holies, into which only the high priest could go, and that only once a year with the sacrifice of atonement. It is not clear which of these curtains was now torn apart, but in either case the symbolism is powerful: the way which was previously closed is now thrown open, and there is free access to the holy place. The violent destruction also points forward to what will happen to the temple as a whole a generation later. With the death of Jesus its whole sacrificial ritual has become obsolete. The fact that the huge curtain, some 60 feet high, is torn from the top to the bottom suggests that this is not a human act.

## A Gentile's testimony

The centurion, a middle-ranking Roman soldier roughly equivalent to our NCO, would be in charge of the execution squad. While the Jewish crowd have been insulting Jesus, this man has been watching him, and what he has seen and heard has moved him to a very different perception to theirs. We do not know what it was about how Jesus died that so impressed him, but his verdict is in striking contrast to their rejection of Jesus' claims. Perhaps he has heard something of Jesus' alleged claim to be 'the Son of God' in a special sense, or perhaps he is simply talking in his natural pagan way about 'a son of God', a good and pious man. Whatever was in his mind, for Mark this is the crowning testimony to the truth of Jesus' claim so powerfully proclaimed before the Sanhedrin. And it is in full accord with Mark's love of paradox that it is in the moment of Jesus' ultimate humiliation and death that he receives this glowing tribute, and that even then it is not from his own people but from one of the pagan occupying forces.

## The witnesses

Mark gives no hint that any of the male disciples were around to see Jesus die, but there were some supporters on the edge of the crowd. The men have run away, and the women take over. It is they who are at the centre of the rest of the story. They form an important chain of witness, as these same women will watch first Jesus' death, then his burial (v. 47), and it will be they who discover that the tomb is empty and to whom the message of the resurrection is entrusted (16:1–8). So there can be no mistake, no allegations about Jesus not being really dead, or about going to the wrong tomb. The same group of women have witnessed the whole thing, and it is on their testimony that the church will forever depend.

### FOR MEDITATION
*We have this hope, a sure and steadfast anchor of the soul, a hope that enters the inner shrine behind the curtain, where Jesus, a forerunner on our behalf, has entered, having become a high priest forever... we have confidence to enter the sanctuary by the blood of Jesus, by the new and living way that he opened for us through the curtain (that is, through his flesh).*
**Hebrews 6:19–20; 10:19–20**

## The sabbath

The Jewish day began and ended at sunset. So the evening of that
Friday would be the beginning of the sabbath. The desire to bury the
body of Jesus before the sabbath began was partly due to the con-
vention that it was not proper for the body to remain publicly
exposed on the sabbath day (or indeed after sunset on any day,
Deuteronomy 21:23). But there was also the practical concern that
the 'work' involved in taking down a body and preparing it for burial would be against accepted sabbath law. It may have been because
of the short time available before sunset that Joseph, for all his care,
apparently omitted to provide the customary spices for the burial
(see 16:1).

The Romans had no such scruples, and clearly expected the crucified men to remain on the crosses through the sabbath day; they
might well still not be dead by the end of it. Hence Pilate's surprise
that Joseph could be contemplating burying Jesus a mere few hours
after he was crucified. Crucified men did not normally die as quickly
as that. But in any case, the Romans would not be concerned about
burial, since one of the more shameful aspects of crucifixion was that
the corpses were normally simply thrown on the ground unburied,
unless their families took them away. Joseph is asking something
quite unusual in proposing to provide proper burial for this criminal.

## Joseph of Arimathea

Who was this brave man who, when none of the male disciples were
there to take action, took it upon himself to ask for Jesus' body? It
was surely a brave act, since even though a dead Jesus could no
longer be a potential revolutionary leader, to be linked publicly with
a crucified 'rebel' was politically dangerous. And of course Joseph
was a Jew, and a highly respected one at that. Yet here he is publicly
taking the part of the man whom his own Sanhedrin has so recently
thrown out as a blasphemer.

He was 'waiting expectantly for the kingdom of God'. So were many Jews, of course, but for Mark the Christian writer to describe him in these terms suggests that, even if he was not a 'signed-up' disciple of Jesus, he was recognized by the church as 'one of us'. Perhaps at this stage he was like the scribe of 12:34, 'not far from the kingdom of God'. But the fact that he was remembered in the Christian stories of Jesus suggests that he was later, if not already, identified as one of Jesus' followers (though we need not believe the medieval legend which brings him to Glastonbury as a Christian missionary!). If so, this is an important hint that Jesus' followers were not all from the fisherman class. Indeed, a man who could provide a rock-cut tomb just outside the city of Jerusalem must have been a very wealthy man.

## The tomb of Jesus

The visitor to Jerusalem can still visit dozens of rock-hewn tombs in and around the city, some of them still with a large stone to roll across the low entrance. Many of them are multiple tombs with spaces for a considerable number of bodies. Perhaps that is why all the other Gospels mention that this was a *new* tomb, with no other bodies, so that there was no possibility of mistake when the tomb was declared to be empty. But in any case Mark makes sure we know that the women who are going to find it empty are the same ones who 'saw where the body was laid'. There is no mistake. We cannot now be sure just where the tomb of Jesus was, but they knew well enough.

So at the end of chapter 15 Jesus is a corpse, wrapped up in tight linen grave-clothes, placed in a tomb and guarded by a great stone. You cannot get much more final than that.

### PRAYER

*Thank you, Lord, for the example of the 'lesser' characters in the Gospel story like Joseph. May we too be ready for any special task we may be called on to perform in your service.*

# 'He is not here'

All four Gospels tell about the finding of the empty tomb early on Sunday morning. The details do not all agree—how many women? which women? the stone already gone or an angel rolling it back? how many angels and where were they? and just what did they say? But these are not the central features of the story, and we can hardly be surprised to find a certain amount of variation in the way a story of such a mind-blowing event was told and passed down. The main points are not in question.

## The tomb is empty

The women, who had seen the body laid there on Friday evening, and who have come expecting to find it still there so that they can complete the burial rites, are specifically invited to look at the place where it should have been. Whatever the explanation, the simple fact is that there is no body.

## The message of resurrection

If we may judge by the parallel accounts in the other Gospels, the young man in white is an angel (white, shining clothes are a feature of stories of angels appearing in the Bible; see also Luke 24:4, and the mention that these men in dazzling clothes were angels in 24:23). He is too well informed to be a passer-by who has just happened to look into the open tomb, and attempts to identify him as any of the disciples are purely speculative, and in any case do not tally with his message which is specifically addressed *to* the disciples. He is a heavenly messenger sent to explain to them why the tomb is empty. Perhaps, after Jesus' predictions that he would rise again, they should have needed no angelic messenger; but even his closest disciples seem not to have grasped what he meant.

# The promise of reunion

But the empty tomb is not an end in itself. It is for the disciples the promise of a living Jesus, and of a new beginning with him. Just as the original mission began and flourished in Galilee, so now it is to Galilee that they must go to meet their risen Lord. Jerusalem, with all its terrible memories, is to be left behind. A new chapter is about to begin.

The message is the same as that which Jesus has already given to the disciples in 14:28, but at that stage they were hardly in a position to take it in. Now that all hope seems to have gone, it is repeated as the dawn of new hope. It is the promise not just that they will rally again and the cause will not die. It is much more specific than that: 'You will see him'!

And the message is not merely to the disciples, but to 'his disciples and Peter'. We can readily imagine what those words would mean to the disciple whom we last saw weeping in failure and despair in the high priest's courtyard.

# The women run away

We can well understand the women's 'terror and amazement'. To go to a tomb looking for a body and to find there a living angel instead of the body would unnerve the strongest of us. What is not so easy to grasp is their fear and their silence. The message they have been given is one of hope and joy, and they have been specifically commissioned to pass it on to the disciples. Does Mark want us to believe that their fear and their silence were only temporary, and that in due course they plucked up courage and delivered the message? Perhaps, but he does not say so. Few books can finish in a more mystifying and unsatisfying way. Unless of course that is not the end—see the next study!

### FOR MEDITATION
*If Christ has not been raised, your faith is futile...*
*If for this life only we have hoped in Christ,*
*we are of all people most to be pitied.*
**1 Corinthians 15:17, 19**

*He is risen indeed. Hallelujah!*

# 107 How did Mark finish his Gospel?

In the last study I referred to 16:8 as the end of Mark's Gospel. But in older Bibles twelve further verses used to be printed after 16:8. Modern versions, however, either do not print these 'verses 9–20' as part of the text of the Gospel at all, or indicate in some way that their status is suspect. With very few exceptions modern scholars agree that verses 9–20 are not part of the original Gospel of Mark. In many early manuscripts and versions these verses are either absent altogether or marked as of doubtful authority. In some early texts an alternative ending appears, either on its own or together with verses 9–20.

## Is this the end?

So how did Mark finish his Gospel? Did he really intend to leave it hanging in the air at verse 8, with the message entrusted to the women but not delivered, and with the puzzling comment that they said nothing to anyone? Many scholars think that he did, that the book is deliberately open-ended, leaving readers to make up their own minds about the riddle of the empty tomb rather than spelling it all out for them. Others feel that that is a very 'modern' (or better 'post-modern'?) way of thinking, and that an early Christian like Mark is likely to have been more concerned with making the gospel message clear and explicit than with achieving a teasing literary effect. In any case, the angel's message in verse 7 is explicit enough—all that is lacking is an account of how it was fulfilled.

If this latter view is right, and 16:8 was not intended to be the end of the story, we have two options. Either Mark intended to go on, but was prevented from finishing his book (and one can only guess what might have prevented him: sudden illness? a knock at the door from the secret police?...). Or he did finish it, and the original end is lost, perhaps through a leaf being torn off the scroll? Matthew, whose account is so closely parallel to Mark's up to this point, goes on to record a meeting of Jesus with the eleven disciples in Galilee, as the angel has predicted (Matthew 28:16–20), and perhaps Mark originally had a similar ending with one or more appearances of the risen Jesus to his disciples.

## Filling the gap

We do not know, and guesses are not very helpful. But the feeling that 16:8 cannot be the intended end is supported by the fact that the 'shorter' and 'longer' endings began to circulate with the Gospel probably some time in the second century. These endings were added because early readers of Mark felt something important was missing. The 'shorter ending' rounds it all off very succinctly, while the 'longer ending' consists of a more substantial collection of traditions about the risen Jesus drawn from the other Gospels, particularly Luke, and from early Christian preaching. The language and style of both endings is clearly different from that of Mark.

There is not much in these later endings which is new or surprising. The one section which is not paralleled elsewhere in the New Testament is the alleged words of Jesus in verses 15–18, with their promise of 'signs' including 'speaking in new tongues' and protection from venomous snakes and poisons. 'Speaking in tongues' was, of course, a feature of some of the early churches, as we know especially from 1 Corinthians 12 and 14. And in Acts 28:3–6 there is an account of Paul surviving the bite of a poisonous snake (though no indication that this was a regular occurrence, still less something to be deliberately encouraged). But it is not wise to base one's understanding of Christian discipleship and mission on this later addition to Mark's Gospel.

### FOR MEDITATION

*If you had been Mark, would you have finished your story at 16:8? What would be missing? Was there really any need for someone to add on a further 'ending'?*

*In what sense, if at all, is it appropriate to think of either or both of the later endings as 'scripture'?*

# 108 Mark's good news— a retrospective

Now that we have reached the end of Mark's story, it is worth while to pause and ask what we have learned from it.

We have learned at least, I hope, to appreciate Mark as a lively, interesting and skilful writer. If you haven't yet had the opportunity to read Mark's whole Gospel at one go, why not find time to do it now, and see how the various episodes and teaching which we have been looking at all come together into an enthralling and powerful story? As you do so, you will notice again the special emphases and interests which make this not just another Gospel, but in a very distinctive way *Mark's* Gospel.

But Mark did not write his book to tell us about himself. It is the good news about *Jesus*, the Messiah, the Son of God (1:1). So what have we learned about Jesus?

It has been a book full of surprises. Jesus is a man of contrasts and of paradox. He attracts both enthusiastic crowds and implacable enemies. He preaches a kingdom of God which is coming with power and yet which is as easily overlooked as a grain of mustard seed. He acts with miraculous power and controls the elements of nature, and yet we see him as weak and vulnerable, sharing our emotions of frustration, anger, and the fear of death. He is revealed on the mountain as a majestic, other-worldly being, and yet we see him unrecognized, mocked, humiliated. He is declared by God's own voice to be his beloved Son, and yet he is one of us, sharing the full range of human experience. He is the Son of man, destined to reign in glory over all the world—and yet also destined to be rejected by his own people, to suffer and to die. He has a unique relationship with God as his father ('Abba'), and yet on the cross he cries out to a God who has abandoned him.

To follow such a master, as Mark clearly longs that we should, is sure to be an equally paradoxical experience, at once exhilarating and humbling, enlightening and bewildering. It is an experience of losing life in order to gain it. As we walk with Jesus' closest disciples through this story we share their excitement as the secret of the kingdom of God is gradually revealed to them, and yet their embarrassment when Jesus declares them to be still as blind as ever. They struggle to keep up with the new values and ideas which he insistently places before them, but again and again they are wrong-footed. They are discovering, sometimes painfully, a whole new world in which the last are first and the first last, the greatest are the lowest and the leader is the servant. They are summoned to take up their cross and follow Jesus, but the end of the road is glory. So we, Mark's readers, are called to join them 'on the road', a road where there is little that is familiar or secure, but a road which leads to life. The road begins with the summons 'Follow me, and I will make you fish for people', but it seems to end at Golgotha—until we hear the angel's message to the eleven disciples through a few frightened women: 'He is going ahead of you; you will see him.'

What a book! What a Messiah! What a calling to follow him!

# NOTES

# NOTES

**PBC voucher MK** 01

# THE PEOPLE'S BIBLE COMMENTARY VOUCHER SCHEME

The People's Bible Commentary (PBC) provides a range of readable, accessible commentaries. These will grow into a library that will eventually cover the whole Bible.

A voucher is printed on the last page of each People's Bible Commentary Volume (as above). These vouchers count towards free copies of other volumes in the series.

• 4 purchases of PBC volumes entitle the reader to a further volume (up to the value of £7.99) FREE

• 6 purchases of PBC volumes entitle the reader to a further volume (up to the value of £9.99) FREE

You should find a coupon for the PBC voucher scheme inserted loose with this volume. If for some reason the coupon is missing, please ask at your local bookshop or contact BRF direct to obtain a replacement.

**All you need do:**

• Cut out the appropriate vouchers from the last page of the PBCs you have purchased and attach them to the coupon.

• Complete your name and address details, and indicate your choice of free entitlement from the list on the coupon.

• Take the coupon to your local Christian Bookshop who will exchange it for your free PBC volume; or send the coupon direct to BRF who will send you your free PBC volume. Please allow 28 days for delivery.

Please note that PBC volumes provided under the voucher scheme are subject to availability. If your first choice is not available, you may be sent your second choice volume.

BRF, Peter's Way, Sandy Lane West, Oxford OX4 5HG
Tel 01865 748227   Fax 01865 773150   Registered Charity No. 233280